A Friendly Introduction to MATLAB Programming

by Prof. Dr. Orhan Gazi

oG Publications

Copyright Information

Orhan Gazi

Electrical and Electronics Engineering Department

Ankara Medipol University

Ankara, Turkey

ISBN: 9798323478491

© oG

oG Publications

This work is subject to copyright. All rights are reserved by the Publisher, whether the whole or part of the material is concerned, specifically the rights of translation, reprinting, reuse of illustrations, recitation, broadcasting, reproduction on microfilms or in any other physical way, and transmission or information storage and retrieval, electronic adaptation, computer software, or by similar or dissimilar methodology now known or hereafter developed. The use of general descriptive names, registered names, trademarks, service marks, etc. in this publication does not imply, even in the absence of a specific statement, that such names are exempt from the relevant protective laws and regulations and therefore free for general use. The publisher, the authors, and the editors are safe to assume that the advice and information in this book are believed to be true and accurate at the date of publication. Neither the publisher nor the authors or the editors give a warranty, expressed or implied, with respect to the material contained herein or for any errors or omissions that may have been made. The publisher remains neutral with regard to jurisdictional claims in published maps and institutional affiliations. This imprint is published by Orhan Gazi.

Preface

MATLAB, i.e., matrix laboratory, is a software tool mostly used by engineers. There are numerous books written about MATLAB. However, for a beginner, we believe that it is still time consuming to find the appropriate book for quick learning of the MATLAB fundamentals. Many books include too much material for MATLAB teaching and this slows down the learning speed of the reader, and the reader can still be unaware of the many simple fundamentals even when they complete reading several books. For instance, many students do homework using MATLAB and they draw many graphs using MATLAB but they still do not know how MATLAB draws the graphs.

In this tutorial we focused on the fundamental concepts of MATLAB programming and tried to teach MATLAB programming basics without going into clumsy coding. We paid attention to the simplicity of the programs and tried to teach the basic concepts directly without being lost among long programing lines.

This book can be used by anyone who wants to learn MATLAB is very short time. In fact, the fundamental concepts explained in this book can be learned in a week. Ch1

In chapter-1 e explain MATLAB commands input, disp, linspace, zeros, and introduce the number vectors and perform operations on number vectors.

Chapter-2 is devoted to matrix operations, loop and conditional structures. Chapter-2 contains the programming side of the MATLAB.

Chapter-3 and 4 focus on graphic drawing with MATLAB. Graphic drawing is one of the most powerful sides of the MATLAB.

Table of Contents

Copyright Information 2

Preface 3

Chapter-1 7

MATLAB Commands-1 7

    1.1 Taking Input from Keyboard 7

    1.2 Data Display on Screen 9

    1.3 Number Vectors 10

    1.4 LINSPACE command 11

    1.5 Indices of the Vector Elements 12

    1.6 Transpose of a Vector 13

    1.7 Zero and One Vectors 14

    1.8 Matrices 15

    1.9 FIND command 20

Chapter-2 21

MATLAB Commands-2 21

    2.1 Matrix Transpose 21

    2.2 Matrix Operations 22

    2.3 MATLAB HELP Function 25

    2.4 LOOKFOR Command 26

    2.5 QUIT and EXIT Commands 26

    2.6 Clc, Clear All and Close All Commands 26

    2.7 SAVE Command 26

    2.8 LOAD Command 28

    2.9 INF and NaN Results 28

    2.10 Who Command 29

    2.11 Complex Numbers in MATLAB 29

    2.12 MATLAB Functions and MATLAB Scripts 30

    2.13 Functions in MATLAB 32

    2.14 Relational and Logical Operations in MATLAB 35

    2.15 Control Flow Statements 37

        If and Break Statements 37

        For Loops 39

    While Loops 40

Chapter-3 42

MATLAB Commands-3 42

  3.1 How to Write MATLAB Programs Which Runs Fast and Use Less Memory: 42

    TIC Command 42

    TOC Command 42

  3.2 Pre Memory Reservation 44

  3.3 Graphics in MATLAB 45

    AXIS Command 48

  3.4 Determination of Coordinates 50

  3.5 HOLD ON Command 56

  3.6 HOLD OFF Command 58

  3.7 XLABEL, YLABEL, and TITLE Commands 59

  3.8 GTEXT Command 62

  3.9 LEGEND Command 64

  3.10 GRIN ON Command 64

Chapter-4 67

MATLAB Commands-4 67

  4.1 STEM Command 67

  4.2 SUBPLOT Command 77

  4.3 FIGURE Command 83

Chapter-1

MATLAB Commands-1

Abstract: In this chapter, we explain the type MATLAB commands input, disp, linspace, zeros, and ones. Besides, we introduce the number vectors and perform operations on number vectors.

1.1 Taking Input from Keyboard

INPUT command

The input command is used to get data from the user and it is used as

```
r = input('Please enter your input: ');
```

where the variable r is used to keep the entered data.

Example-1.1:

```
Command Window
>> r=input('Please enter and integer: ')
Please enter and integer: 23

r =

    23
```

Figure-1.1 The use of input command

If we just hit the return key without entering a value, then empty matrix is assigned to the variable as shown in Figure-1.2

```
Command Window
>> r=input('Please enter and integer: ')
Please enter and integer:

r =

    []
```

Figure-1.2 The use of input command

If the input data is a string, then the input command is used as

$$r = \text{input}('Please\ enter\ your\ name:\ ',\ 's');$$

Example-1.2:

```
Command Window
>> r=input('Please enter your name: ', 's')
Please enter your name: Ohan

r =

    'Ohan'
```

Figure-1.3

In Figure-1.3, we did not use semicolon after the first line that is why the variable name, i.e., r and its name is displayed. If we use a semicolon at the end of the first line, then nothing is displayed as shown in Figure-1.4.

Example-1.3:

```
Command Window
>> r=input('Please enter your name: ', 's');
Please enter your name: Ohan
>>
```

Figure-1.4

We can use the next line operator '\n' inside a text to break it into two parts as shown in Figure-1.5

Example-1.4:

```
Command Window
>> r=input('Please enter\nyour name: ', 's');
Please enter
your name: Ohan
>>
```

Figure-1.5

1.2 Data Display on Screen

DISP command

The command disp() is used to print the values and results to the monitor, an it is used as

$$\text{disp}(X)$$

where X can be number vector, or it can be a matrix, or it can be a string.

Example-1.5:

```
Command Window
>> disp('Hello world, how are you?');
Hello world, how are you?
>>
```

Figure-1.6

Example-1.6:

```
Command Window
>> x=[2 3 6 7 8 -2 -5 6];
>> disp(x);
     2     3     6     7     8    -2    -5     6

>>
```

Figure-1.7

1.3 Number Vectors

A number vector can be formed as in

$x = [2.3 \quad 4.5 \quad 6 - 5.6 \quad 7]$.

We can also use the colon operator, **:**, to generate the vector elements as

$x = first\ element{:}increment\ amount{:}last\ element$

Example-1.7:

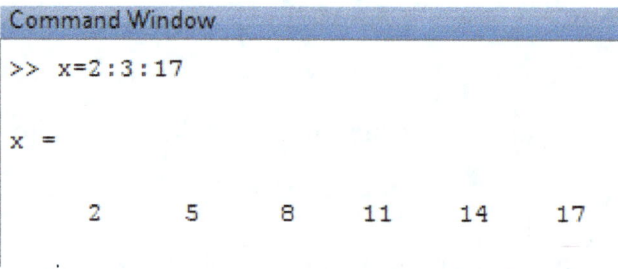

Figure-1.8

Increment amount can be a negative number

Example-1.8:

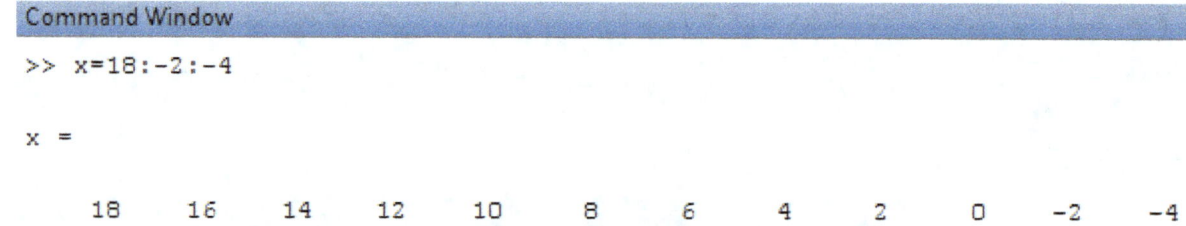

Figure-1.9

Multiplication of Two Vectors

Let

$x = [x_1\ x_2 \cdots x_N]$

and

$y = [y_1\ y_2 \cdots y_N]$

be two number vectors. The dot product of these two vectors is calculated using

$$x.*y = [x_1y_1 \ x_2y_2 \cdots x_Ny_N]$$

Example-1.9:

```
Command Window
>> x=[2 3 5 7];
>> y=[2 2 2 2];
>> x.*y

ans =

     4     6    10    14
```

Figure-1.10

Number vectors can be used as arguments of functions, in this case the function operates on each of the vector elements.

Example-1.10: For $x = [2 \ -4 \ 6 \ 1.2 \ 4]$, $y = \exp(x)$ gives

$y = [\exp(2) \ \exp(-4) \ \exp(6) \ \exp(1.2) \ \exp(4)]$

Example-1.11:

```
Command Window
>> x=0:pi/4:2*pi;
>> y=sin(x)

y =

     0    0.7071    1.0000    0.7071    0.0000   -0.7071   -1.0000   -0.7071   -0.0000
```

Figure-1.11

Note: In MATLAB pi is used for π.

1.4 LINSPACE command

Linspace command is used to generate a number vector between two numbers. It is used as

```
r = linspace(first_number, last_number, N);
```

where N is the length of the vector, and the vector contains the first and last numbers as well.

Example-1.12:

```
Command Window
>> r=linspace(-4,4,5)

r =

    -4    -2     0     2     4
```

Figure-1.12

Example-1.13:

```
Command Window
>> r=linspace(-pi,pi,8)

r =

  -3.1416  -2.2440  -1.3464  -0.4488   0.4488   1.3464   2.2440   3.1416
```

Figure-1.13

1.5 Indices of the Vector Elements

For the number vector $x = [x_1\, x_2 \cdots x_N]$ the first element is x_1 and the index of the first element is 1, and the last element is x_N and the index of the last element is N. The ith element of the vector x is $x(i)$.

Example-1.14:

```
Command Window
>> x=[-4 6 8 9 3 -3 4 7 0];
>> x(3), x(7)

ans =

     8


ans =

     4
```

Figure-1.14

The expression

$x(i:j)$

indicates the sub-vector obtained from x with the indices $i, i+1, \cdots, j$.

The expression

$x(i:k:j)$

indicates the sub-vector obtained from x with the indices $i, i+k, i+2k, \cdots, j$.

Example-1.15:

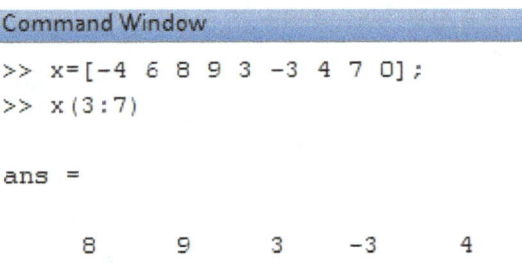

Figure-1.15

Example-1.16:

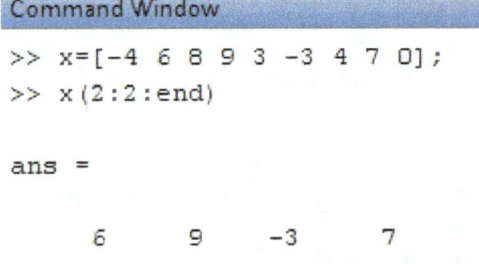

Figure-1.16

1.6 Transpose of a Vector

The transpose of the vector x is obtained either using x' or using transpose(x).

Example-1.17:

```
Command Window
>> x=[-4 6 8 9];
>> x'

ans =

    -4
     6
     8
     9

>> transpose(x)

ans =

    -4
     6
     8
     9
```

Figure-1.17

1.7 Zero and One Vectors

We can generate zero and one vector containing N zeros and N ones using

        zeros(1, N)   and **ones**(1, N)

Example-1.18:

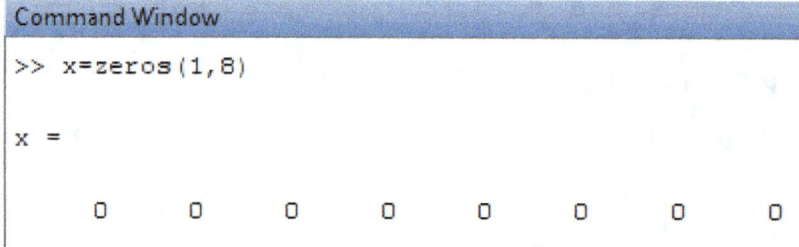

Figure-1.18

Example-1.19:

```
Command Window
>> x=ones(1,8)

x =

     1     1     1     1     1     1     1     1
```

Figure-1.19

1.8 Matrices

A matrix of size 3×3 is defined as

$A = [1\ \ 2\ \ 3; 4\ \ 5\ \ 6; 7\ \ 8\ \ 9]$

Where each row of the matrix is separated with semicolon, i.e., ;

Example-1.20:

```
Command Window
>> A=[1 2 3; 4 5 6; 7 8 9]

A =

     1     2     3
     4     5     6
     7     8     9
```

Figure-1.20

Elements of a Matrix

Let A denote a matrix. The rows of A can be obtained as in

$A(1,:)\rightarrow$ indicates the first row of the matrix

$A(3,:)\rightarrow$ indicates the third row of the matrix

$A(j,:)\rightarrow$ indicates the jth row of the matrix

Example-1.21:

```
Command Window
>> A=[1 2 3; 4 5 6; 7 8 9]

A =

     1     2     3
     4     5     6
     7     8     9

>> A(1,:)

ans =

     1     2     3
```

```
Command Window
>> A=[1 2 3; 4 5 6; 7 8 9]

A =

     1     2     3
     4     5     6
     7     8     9

>> A(3,:)

ans =

     7     8     9
```

Figure-1.21

The columns of A can be obtained as in

$A(:,1) \rightarrow$ indicates the first column of the matrix

$A(:,3) \rightarrow$ indicates the third column of the matrix

$A(:,j) \rightarrow$ indicates the jth column of the matrix

Example-1.22:

```
Command Window
>> A=[1 2 3; 4 5 6; 7 8 9]

A =

     1     2     3
     4     5     6
     7     8     9

>> A(:,1)

ans =

     1
     4
     7
```

```
Command Window
>> A=[1 2 3; 4 5 6; 7 8 9]

A =

     1     2     3
     4     5     6
     7     8     9

>> A(:,3)

ans =

     3
     6
     9
```

Figure-1.22

$A(2:4,:) \rightarrow$ indicates the submatrix obtained from the rows with row numbers 2, 3, and 4

$A(:,1:3) \rightarrow$ indicates the submatrix obtained from the columns with column numbers 1, 2, and 3

$A(1:3, 2:4) \rightarrow$ indicates the submatrix obtained from the intersection of rows 1, 2, 3 and columns 2, 3, 4

$A(a:b,c:d) \rightarrow$ indicates the submatrix obtained from the intersection of rows $a, a+1, \cdots, b$ and columns $c, c+1, \cdots, d$

$A(a:k:b,c:m:d) \rightarrow$ indicates the submatrix obtained from the intersection of rows $a, a+k, \cdots, b$ and columns $c, c+m, \cdots, d$

$A(:) \rightarrow$ indicates the matrix obtained by concatenating the columns of A

Example-1.23:

```
Command Window
>> A=[1 2 3 4; 5 6 7 8; 9 10 11 12; 13 14 15 16]

A =

     1     2     3     4
     5     6     7     8
     9    10    11    12
    13    14    15    16
```

Figure-1.23

Example-1.24:

```
Command Window
>> A=[1 2 3 4; 5 6 7 8; 9 10 11 12; 13 14 15 16]

A =

     1     2     3     4
     5     6     7     8
     9    10    11    12
    13    14    15    16

>> A(2:4,:)

ans =

     5     6     7     8
     9    10    11    12
    13    14    15    16
```

Figure-1.24

Example-1.25:

```
Command Window
>> A=[1 2 3 4; 5 6 7 8; 9 10 11 12; 13 14 15 16]

A =

     1     2     3     4
     5     6     7     8
     9    10    11    12
    13    14    15    16

>> A(:,1:3)

ans =

     1     2     3
     5     6     7
     9    10    11
    13    14    15
```

Figure-1.25

Example-1.26:

```
Command Window
>> A=[1 2 3 4; 5 6 7 8; 9 10 11 12; 13 14 15 16]

A =

     1     2     3     4
     5     6     7     8
     9    10    11    12
    13    14    15    16

>> A(1:3,2:4)

ans =

     2     3     4
     6     7     8
    10    11    12
```

Figure-1.26

Example-1.27:

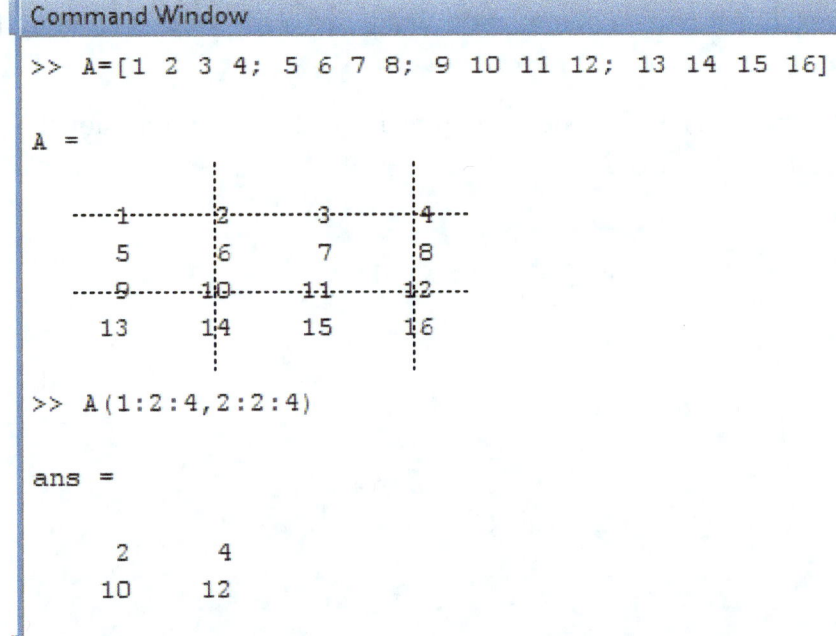

Figure-1.27

Example-1.28:

```
Command Window
>> A=[1 2 3; 4 5 6]

A =

     1     2     3
     4     5     6

>> A(:)

ans =

     1
     4
     2
     5
     3
     6
```

Figure-1.28

1.9 FIND command

Find command is used to get the one dimensional index of a matrix element. Order indexes start from the first element of the first column and it increases downward continuing from the second column and so on.

Example-1.29: In the MATLAB code in Figure-1.29, the one dimensional indices of matrix element 5 are found and displayed

```
Command Window
>> A=[5 4 7; 8 0 5]

A =

     5     4     7
     8     0     5

>> find(A==5)

ans =

     1
     6
```

Figure-1.29

Example-1.30: In the MATLAB code in Figure-1.30, the one dimensional indices of matrix elements greater than or equal to 5 are found and displayed

```
Command Window
>> A=[5 4 7; 8 0 5]

A =

     5     4     7
     8     0     5

>> find(A>=5)

ans =

     1
     2
     5
     6
```

Figure-1.30

Chapter-2

MATLAB Commands-2

Abstract: In this chapter, we first perform operations of matrices, and then explain the commands help, lookfor, quit, exit, clc, close all, clear all, save, load, who. After studying logical operations with MATLAB, we will explain loop and control structures in MATLAB programming.

2.1 Matrix Transpose

The matrix obtained by replacing the rows of a matrix with columns and the columns with rows is called a transpose matrix. If the matrix A is defined as

$$A = \begin{bmatrix} a_{11} & \cdots & a_{k1} \\ \vdots & \ddots & \vdots \\ a_{1n} & \cdots & a_{kn} \end{bmatrix}$$

then the transpose matrix happens to be as

$$A^T = \begin{bmatrix} a_{11} & \cdots & a_{1n} \\ \vdots & \ddots & \vdots \\ a_{k1} & \cdots & a_{kn} \end{bmatrix}.$$

In MATLAB the transpose of A is obtained using either A' or $transpose(A)$.

Example-2.1:

```
Command Window
>> A=[5 4 7; 8 0 5]

A =

     5     4     7
     8     0     5

>> transpose(A)

ans =

     5     8
     4     0
     7     5
```

```
Command Window
>> A=[5 4 7; 8 0 5]

A =

     5     4     7
     8     0     5

>> A'

ans =

     5     8
     4     0
     7     5
```

Figure-2.1

2.2 Matrix Operations

Let A and B be two matrices as

$$A = \begin{bmatrix} a_{11} & \cdots & a_{k1} \\ \vdots & \ddots & \vdots \\ a_{1n} & \cdots & a_{kn} \end{bmatrix} \quad B = \begin{bmatrix} b_{11} & \cdots & b_{k1} \\ \vdots & \ddots & \vdots \\ b_{1n} & \cdots & b_{kn} \end{bmatrix}$$

where n, k are integers. We can perform arithmetic operations with matrices as

$A * B \rightarrow$ is the matrix product of A and B

$A.*B \rightarrow$ is the element product of A and B, that is $A.*B$ is calculated as

$$A.*B = \begin{bmatrix} a_{11}b_{11} & \cdots & a_{k1}b_{k1} \\ \vdots & \ddots & \vdots \\ a_{1n}b_{1n} & \cdots & a_{kn}b_{kn} \end{bmatrix}$$

$k*A \rightarrow$ every element of A is multiplied by k, and a new matrix is formed

$A/k \rightarrow$ every element of A is divided by k, and a new matrix is formed

$A.\wedge k \rightarrow$ the kth power of every element of A is evaluated and a power matrix is formed

$k.\wedge A \rightarrow$ the powers of k are calculated using the elements of the matrix A, and a new matrix is formed

$sin(A) \rightarrow$ the sine of every element of A is calculated, and a new matrix is formed

$\exp(A) \rightarrow$ the exponent of every element of a is calculated, and a new matrix is formed

$g(A) \rightarrow$ the elements of the matrix A are sent to the function $g(\cdot)$ and a new matrix is formed from function returns

$A + B \rightarrow$ is the matrix obtained from the addition of A and B

$A - B \rightarrow$ is the matrix obtained from the subtraction of A and B

Let A and B be two square matrices of the same size, then we have the arithmetic operations

$A/B \rightarrow A$ is divided to B and the result equals AB^{-1}

$A \backslash B \rightarrow B$ is divided to A and the result equals $A^{-1}B$

$inv(A) \rightarrow$ is the inverse of A

$det(A) \rightarrow$ is the determinant of A

Example-2.2: For the matrices A and B given in Figure-2.2

```
Command Window
>> A=[1 2;3 4], B=[5 6;7 8]

A =

     1     2
     3     4


B =

     5     6
     7     8
```

Figure-2.2

We can perform the operations in Example-2.3, 2.4, 2.5, 2.6

Example-2.3:

```
>> A.*B                >> A*B                 >> 2*A

ans =                  ans =                  ans =

     5    12                19    22                2    4
    21    32                43    50                6    8
```

```
>> A/2

ans =

    0.5000    1.0000
    1.5000    2.0000
```

Example-2.4:

```
>> A.^2        >> 3.^A        >> exp(A)              >> sin(A)

ans =          ans =          ans =                  ans =

    1    4        3    9        2.7183    7.3891        0.8415    0.9093
    9   16       27   81       20.0855   54.5982        0.1411   -0.7568
```

Example- 2.5

```
>> inv(A)                    >> det(A)

ans =                        ans =

   -2.0000    1.0000             -2
    1.5000   -0.5000
```

Example-2.6:

```
>> A/B                 >> A\B

ans =                  ans =

    3.0000   -2.0000       -3    -4
    2.0000   -1.0000        4     5
```

2.3 MATLAB HELP Function

MATLAB help function is used as

```
help search_word
```

Example-2.7:

```
Command Window
>> help exp
 EXP    Exponential.
    EXP(X) is the exponential of the elements of X, e to the X.
    For complex Z=X+i*Y, EXP(Z) = EXP(X)*(COS(Y)+i*SIN(Y)).

    See also expm1, log, log10, expm, expint.
```

Figure-2.3

If we type

```
help lang
```

we get the list of programming commands used to write a MATLAB program.

Example-2.8:

```
Command Window
>> help lang
 Programming language constructs.

 Control flow.
    if          - Conditionally execute statements.
    else        - Execute statement if previous IF condition failed.
    elseif      - Execute if previous IF failed and condition is true.
    end         - Terminate scope of control statements.
    for         - Repeat statements a specific number of times.
    parfor      - Parallel FOR-loop.
    while       - Repeat statements an indefinite number of times.
```

Figure-2.4

2.4 LOOKFOR Command

The command lookfor is used to find the terms where the search word is found. It is used as

$$\texttt{lookfor search\_word}$$

Example-2.9:

```
Command Window
>> lookfor inverse
invhilb                    - Inverse Hilbert matrix.
ipermute                   - Inverse permute array dimensions.
acos                       - Inverse cosine, result in radians.
acosd                      - Inverse cosine, result in degrees.
acosh                      - Inverse hyperbolic cosine.
acot                       - Inverse cotangent, result in radian.
```

Figure-2.5

2.5 QUIT and EXIT Commands

To terminate the MATLAB compiler we use quit and exit commands.

2.6 Clc, Clear All and Close All Commands

clc is used to clear the screen, clear all is used to erase all the variables from the memory, and close all is used to close all the open windows.

We usually place all these commands at the beginning of a MATLAB program.

2.7 SAVE Command

When MATLAB is closed all the variables are erased from memory. If we want to save the values of some variables, we can use the save command as

$$\texttt{save file\_name variableName1 variableName2 ...}$$

where file_name is the file in which variable values are stored.

Example-2.10:

```
Command Window
>> x=13.7; y=32.3; z=-23;
>> x

x =

    13.7000

>> y

y =

    32.3000

>> z

z =

   -23
```

Figure-2.6

Example-2.11:

```
Command Window
>> x=13.7; y=32.3; z=-23;
>> clear all;
>> x
??? Undefined function or variable 'x'.

>> y
??? Undefined function or variable 'y'.

>> z
??? Undefined function or variable 'z'.
```

Figure-2.7

Example-2.12:

```
Command Window
>> x=13.7; y=32.3; z=-23;
>> save myVariables x y z
>> dir *.mat

myVariables.mat
```

Figure-2.8

Example-2.13:

```
Command Window
>> x=13.7; y=32.3; z=-23;
>> save myVariables x y z
>> clear all;
>> x
Undefined function or variable 'x'.
```

Figure-2.9

2.8 LOAD Command

Load command is used to restore the previously save variables and their values. It is used as

$$\texttt{load file\_name}$$

Example-2.14:

```
Command Window
>> x=13.7; y=32.3; z=-23;
>> save myVariables x y z
>> clear all;
>> x
Undefined function or variable 'x'.

>> load myVariables
>> x

x =

    13.7000
```

Figure-2.10

We can write simulation programs using MATLAB and after running these simulation programs we can save the results using the save command. Later on we can recover the results using the load command.

2.9 INF and NaN Results

If a number is divided by 0 in MATLAB, we get INF, i.e., infinity, result. The result NaN, i.e., not a number is obtained when $0/0$ or ∞/∞ operations are performed.

Example-2.15:

```
Command Window
>> 1/0

ans =

    Inf

>> 0/0

ans =

    NaN
```

Figure-2.11

2.10 Who Command

The list of defined variables is displayed using who command and it is used as

```
who
```

Example-2.16:

```
Command Window
>> clear all;
>> x=3; y=9; z=2;
>> who

Your variables are:

x  y  z
```

Figure-2.12

2.11 Complex Numbers in MATLAB

We can form the complex numbers in MATLAB using either 'i' or 'j' complex numbers.

Example-2.17:

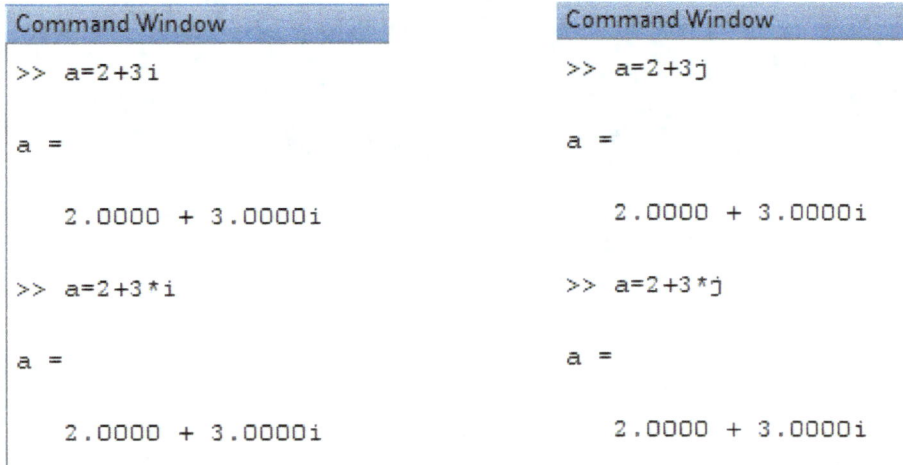

Figure-2.13

Example-2.18:

```
>> a=[1 2; 3 4]+j*[5 6; 7 8]

a =

   1.0000 + 5.0000i   2.0000 + 6.0000i
   3.0000 + 7.0000i   4.0000 + 8.0000i
```

Figure-2.14

2.12 MATLAB Functions and MATLAB Scripts

We write MATLAB programs to files to save them for later use. These files are called script files. MATLAB functions are also written separate files and MATLAB functions can be called inside MATLAB scripts.

At the beginning of a MATLAB script it is custom to write some comment lines to provide information about the written script, and we usually place *clc, clear all,* and *close all* command to the beginning of the program.

Example-2.19: In Figure-2.15 it is shown that to open a new script file we click on the left top icon of the MATLAB platform.

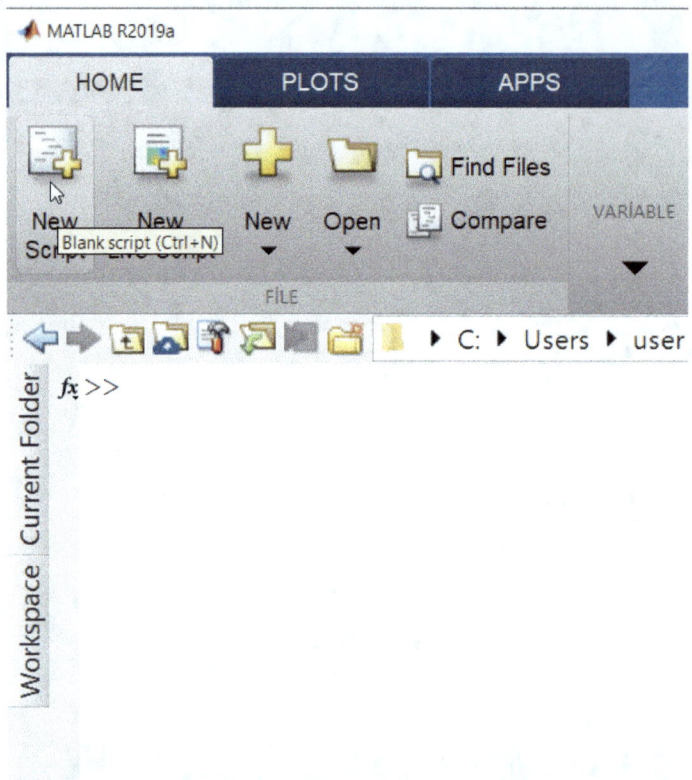

Figure-2.15

Example-2.20: The comment lines can be written as in Figure-2.16 to provide information about the MATLAB code.

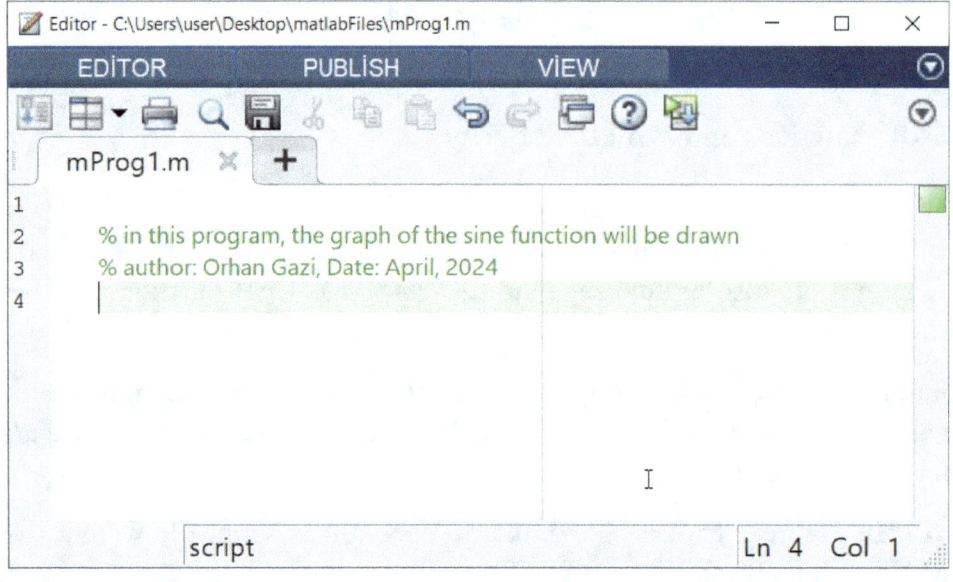

Figure-2.16

Unless otherwise indicated, we will write our programs to MATLAB files from this point on.

2.13 Functions in MATLAB

The template of a MATLAB function is as

```
function [out1, out2, ...] = functionName(inp1, inp2,...)

 % statements
 % statements
  .
  .

  out1 = ..,
  out2 = ..,
```

When the function file is saved, the file name must be the same as the function name, otherwise we cannot call the function inside a script.

Example-2.21:

```
function [ret1, ret2] = sumAndDiff(number1, number2)

% this function finds
% the sum and difference of two numbers

ret1 = number1+number2;
ret2 = number1-number2;
```

Figure-2.17

The function in Example-2.21 can be called as sumAndDiff(45, 7) as in Example-2.22

Example-2.22:

```
Command Window
>> [s, d]=sumAndDiff(45, 7)

s =

    52


d =

    38
```

Figure-2.18

It is also possible to define sub-functions inside a function file, and sub-functions can be called inside the main functions. The template is as

```
function [out1, out2, ...] = mainFunctionName(inp1, inp2,...)
    % statements
    .
    .
    .
    out1 = ..,
    out2 = ..,

function [sub_out1, sub_out2, ...]=subFunctionName1(inp3, inp4,...)
    % statements
    .
    .
    .
    sub_out1 = ..,
    sub_out2 = ..,

function [sub_out3, sub_out4, ...]=subFunctionName2(inp5, inp6,...)
    % statements
    .
    .        .
    .
    sub_out3 = ..,
    sub_out4 = ..,
```

Example-2.23:

```
C:\Users\user\Desktop\matlabFiles\smDfSq.m

EDITOR        PUBLISH        VIEW

1
2    function [sm, df, sqSm, sqDf]=smDfSq(num1, num2)
3      sm =num1 + num2;
4      df = num1 - num2;
5      sqSm = squareSum(num1, num2);
6      sqDf = squareDiff(num1, num2);
7    end
8
9    function ret1 = squareSum(num1, num2)
10     ret1 = num1^2 + num2^2;
11   end
12
13   function ret2 = squareDiff(num1, num2)
14     ret2 = num1^2 - num2^2;
15   end
```

Figure-2.19

```
Command Window
>> smDfSq(1, 2)

ans =

    3

>> [a, b, c, d]=smDfSq(1, 2)

a =

    3

b =

   -1

c =

    5

d =

   -3
```

2.14 Relational and Logical Operations in MATLAB

Relational operators in MATLAB is listed as

    <   →   smaller than

    <=   →   smaller than or equal to

    >   →   greater than

    >=   →   greater than or equal to

    ==   →   equality check

    ~=   →   non equality check

Logical operations in MATLAB are done using

    &   →   logical AND

| → logica OR

~ → logical NOT

$any(x)$ → this function returns '1' for the element of x greater than or equal to zero, otherwise it returns '0' for the corresponding element.

$all(x)$ → this function returns '1' if all the elements of x are greater than or equal to zero, otherwise it returns '0'.

Example-2.24:

```
Command Window
>> x=[4.5 6 7 -2 5 -6 0];
>> x>3

ans =

     1     1     1     0     1     0     0

>> x==7

ans =

     0     0     1     0     0     0     0
```

Figure-2.20

Example-2.25: Let x be a number vector. Find the number of elements of x greater then 5.

```
Command Window
>> x=[3 8 4 7 12 -4 5];
>> y=x>5

y =

     0     1     0     1     1     0     0

>> sum(y)

ans =

     3
```

Figure-2.21

2.15 Control Flow Statements

In MATLAB control flow statements can be written using *for-loops*, *while-loops*, and *if-then-else* structures..

If and Break Statements

The if conditional statement is used as

```
if conditions
    % statements
elseif conditions
    % statements
else
    % statements
end
```

Example-2.26:

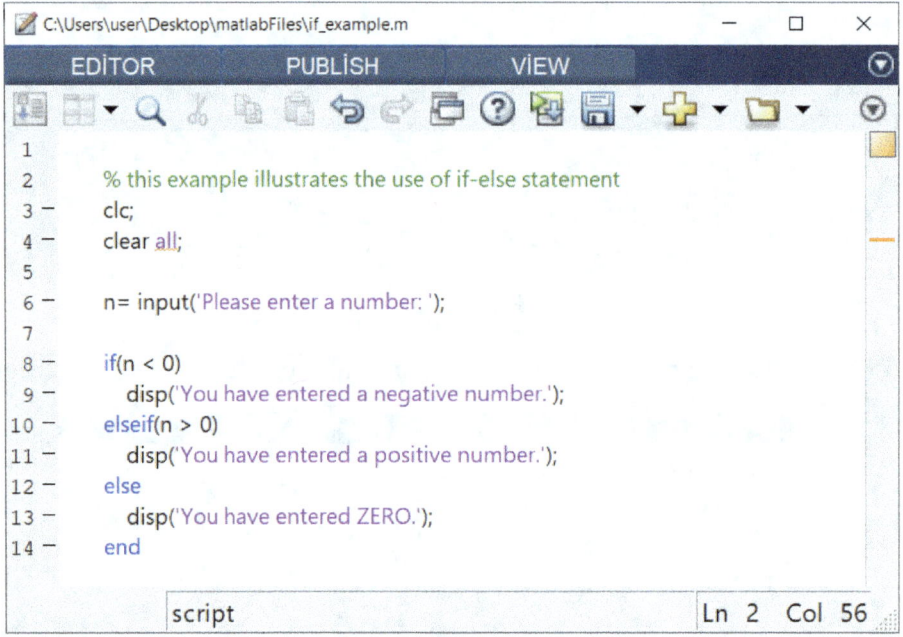

Figure-2.22

When the program in Figure-2.22 is run, we get the output in Figure-2.23.

```
Command Window
Please enter a number: -23
You have entered a negative number.
>>
```

Figure-2.23

Example-2.27: Write a MATLAB program which assigns letter grades to the student marks according to the table.

Letter Grade	Average Mark
AA	> 90
BA	$85 \leq Not < 90$
BB	$80 \leq Not < 85$
CB	$75 \leq Not < 80$
CC	$70 \leq Not < 75$
DC	$65 \leq Not < 70$
DD	$60 \leq Not < 65$
FD	<60

Solution-2.27: The MATLAB program can be written as

```matlab
% clear all;
clc;
mark = input ('Please enter your mark: ');

if (mark > 90)
   letterGrade='AA';
elseif (mark >= 85)
   letterGrade=' BA';
elseif (mark >= 80)
   letterGrade=' BB';
elseif (mark >= 75)
   letterGrade='CB';
elseif(mark >= 70)
   letterGrade='CC';
elseif (mark >= 65)
   letterGrade='DC';
elseif (mark >= 60)
   letterGrade='DD';
else
   letterGrade='FD';
end

disp(['Letter Grade: ' letterGrade]);
```

Figure-2.24

When the MATLAB program in Figure-2.24 is executed we can get an output as in Figure-2.25.

```
Command Window
    Please enter your mark: 56
    Letter Grade: FD
    >>
```

Figure-2.25

For Loops

For loops are used to execute a number of statements for a definite number of times. It is used as

```
for index = values
   % statements
end
```

Example-2.28: Write a MATLAB program which sums the integers from 1 to 9 and displays the result.

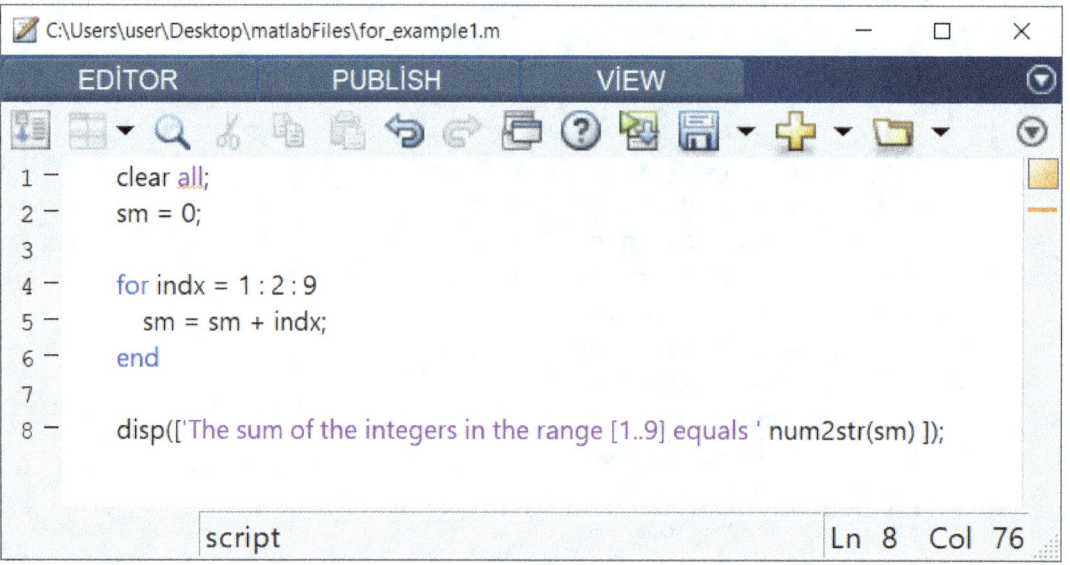

Figure-2.26

When the MATLAB program in Figure-2.26 is run we get the output in Figure-2.27

```
Command Window
>> for_example1
The sum of the integers in the range [1..9] equals 25
>>
```

Figure-2.27

Example-2.29: Write a MATLAB program which finds the sum of the elements of the number vector $a = [1\ 3\ 12\ 6\ 8]$

Solution-2.29: The MATLAB program can be written as in

```
clc; clear all;
sm = 0;

for a = [1 3 12 6 8]
    sm = sm + a;
end
```

When the MATLAB program is executed we obtain the output 30.

While Loops

While loop is written as

```
while logical_condition
    % statements
end
```

where as long as the logical condition is true the statements inside the while-loop are executed, otherwise the loop is quitted.

Example-2.30: Write a MATLAB program which gets a number from the user and concatenates it to the end of a positive number vector, when the user enters a negative number the program quits.
Initially the number vector contains no element.

Solution-2.30: The program can be written as shown in Figure-2.28

```
clc; clear all;

x = [];  % empty vector

n = input('Bir pozitif sayi giriniz: ');

while (n > 0)
    % only positive numbers are considered
    x = [x n] ;
    n = input('Please enter a positive number: ');
end

x   % dislay vector
```

Figure-2.28

When the MATLAB program in Figure-2.28 is run we get an output as in Figure-2.29.

```
Command Window
Bir pozitif sayi giriniz: 5
Please enter a positive number: 67
Please enter a positive number: 23
Please enter a positive number: -1

x =

     5    67    23
```

Figure-2.29

Exercise: Write a program which gets an integer N from the user and displays the vector

$$1\ 2\ 2\ 3\ 3\ 3\ 4\ 4\ 4\ 4\ \underbrace{\ldots\ N\ N\ N\ N}_{N\text{ pieces}}$$

Chapter-3

MATLAB Commands-3

Abstract: In this chapter, first we will explain how to measure the execution speed of the MATLAB programs, and we will show the methods to increase the execution speed of the MATLAB programs. Next, we will explain the MATLAB graphic commands such as plot, axis, hold on, hold off, xlabel, ylabel, grid on, grid off, gtext, and legend.

3.1 How to Write MATLAB Programs Which Runs Fast and Use Less Memory:

If MATLAB programs contains loops statements like for, while, the speed of the programs will be slower. To increase the speed of programs we can replace loop statements by vectors.

TIC Command

It is used to reset the chronometer of MATLAB.

TOC Command

It is used to read the chronometer value of MATLAB.

Example-3.1: The MATLAB program in Figure-3.1 measures the elapsed time needed for the execution of the for loop.

```
1    % example for tic, toc commands
2
3 -  clc; clear all;
4 -  indx = 0;
5
6 -  tic;
7
8 -  for t = 0:0.01:100
9 -      indx=indx+1;
10-      y(indx) =cos (t) ;
11-  end
12
13-  toc;
```

Figure-3.1

When the MATLAB program in Figure-3.1 is run we get an output as in Figure-3.2.

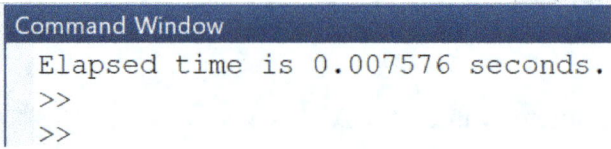

Figure-3.2

We can write the program in Figure-3.1 using vectors as in Figure-3.3.

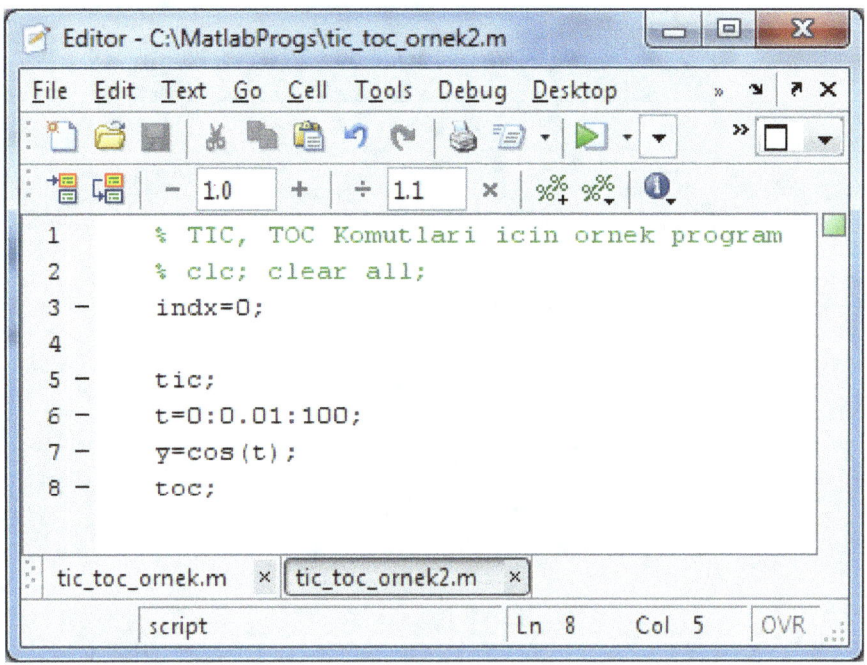

Figure-3.3

When the MATLAB program in Figure-3.3 is run we get an output as in Figure-3.4.

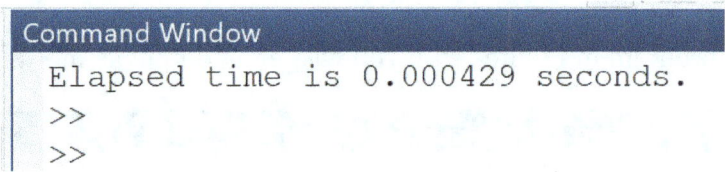

Figure-3.4

The for-loop in Figure-3.1 takes 0.007576 seconds execution time, on the other hand the program in Figure-3.3 takes 0.000429 seconds execution time. It is seen that the second program runs faster.

3.2 Pre Memory Reservation

If the use of loop statements is mandatory in a MATLAB program, to increase the speed of program execution, we can define vectors whose elements equal to zero or one. This is called pre-memory reservation.

Example-3.2: Let's write the program in Figure-3.1 as in Figure-3.5.

```
% clc; clear all;
indx = 0;
y= zeros(1, 10001);

tic;

for t = 0:0.01:100;
    indx = indx+1;
    y(indx) =cos (t) ;
end

toc;
```

Figure-3.5

When the MATLAB program in Figure-3.5 is run we get an output as in Figure-3.6.

```
>> ticToc_example3
Elapsed time is 0.001285 seconds.
>>
```

Figure-3.6

The MATLAB program in Figure-3.1 takes 0.007576 second for execution, and in Figure-3.6 pre-allocation is performed for the same code and the execution time deceased to 0.001285.

It is seen that pre-allocation increase the speed of the program.

3.3 Graphics in MATLAB

To draw the graphs of continuous time signals we use the MATLAB function *plot()*, and to draw the graph of discrete time signals we use the MATLAB function stem(). The *plot()* function is used as

$$plot(x, y)$$

where x and y are two number vectors. Let x=[1 2 3 4] and y=[2 4 5 8], then *plot(x, y)* first locates the coordinates as in Figure-3.7

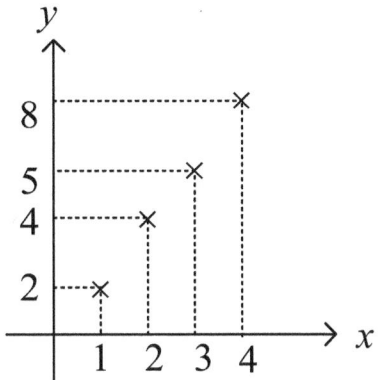

Figure-3.7

and then connects the coordinates and draws the graph as in Figure-3.8.

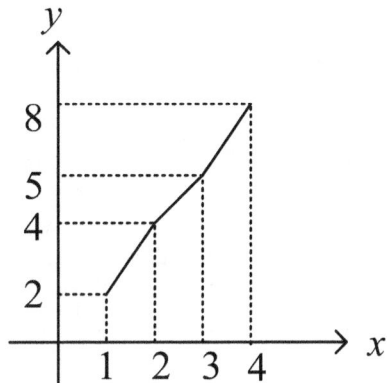

Figure-3.8

Example-3.3: The MATLAB program in Figure-3.9 illustrates the use of plot() function.

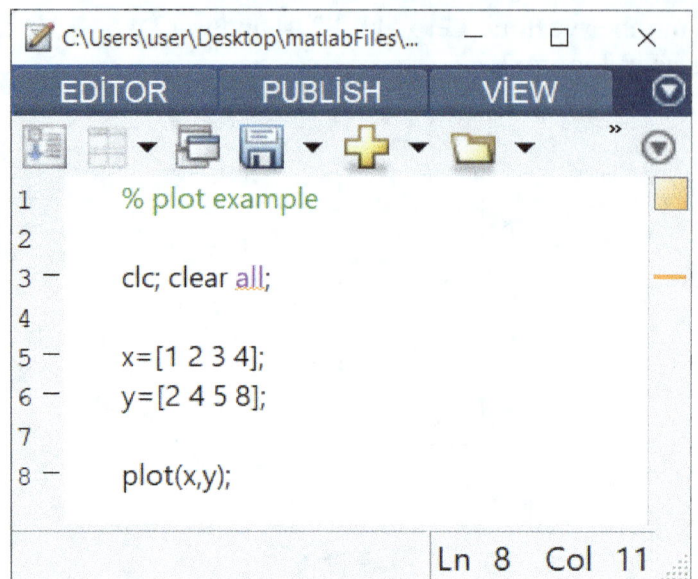

Figure-3.9

When the MATLAB program in Figure-3.9 is run we get an output as in Figure-3.10.

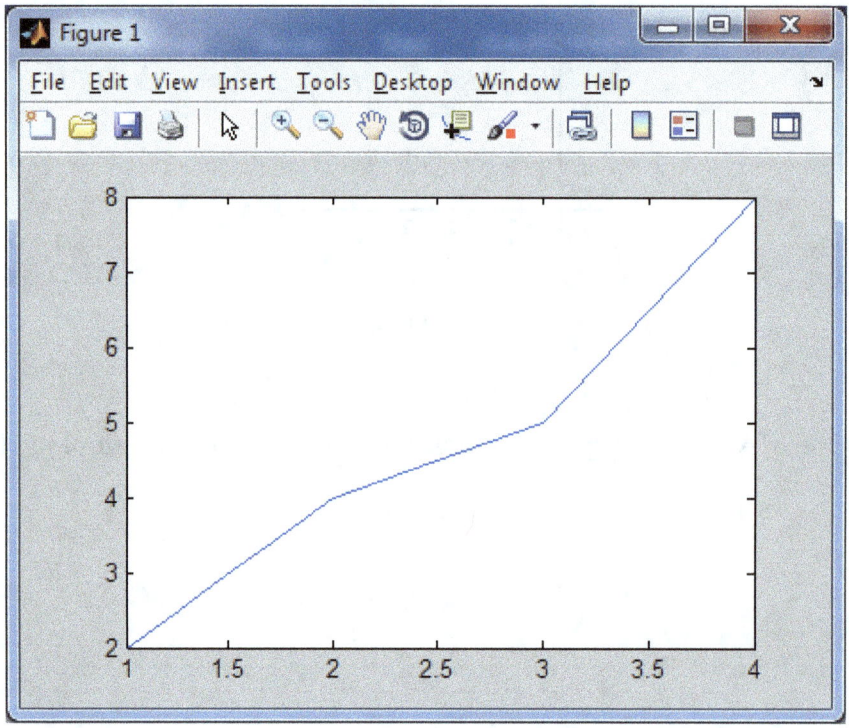

Figure-3.10

If the graph in Figure 3-10 is examined, it is seen that the horizontal axis starts from the integer 1 and the vertical axis starts from the integer 2. The '1' is the first element of the *x* vector and the '2' is the first element of the *y* vector. We can see the graph more clearly by zooming the shape outwards, and for this purpose we can use the "*axis*" command.

If the plot command is used only as '*plot(y)*', then MATLAB accepts the vector *x* as its default value *x*=[1 2 3···] and runs the '*plot(x, y)*' command. In other words, it creates the coordinates of the elements of the *y* vector according to their sequence numbers and draws the graph.

AXIS Command

The axis command is used to zoom a specific part of the graph between certain horizontal and vertical axis values. The general usage of the axis command is as

$$axis([x_{min} \ x_{max} \ y_{min} \ y_{max}])$$

where x_{min} x_{max} and y_{min} y_{max} specify the frontiers of the region to be displayed

Example-3.4:

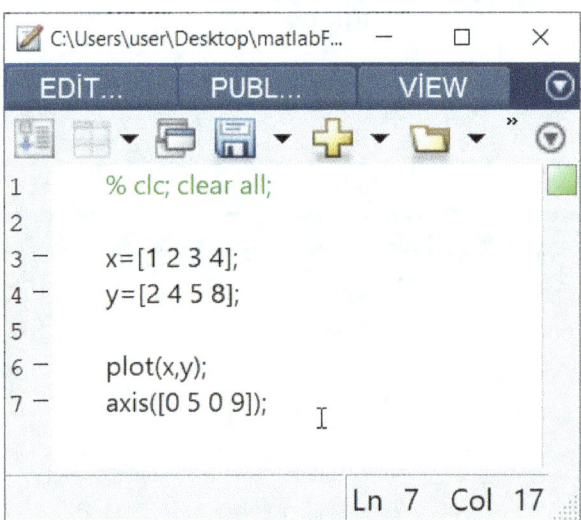

Figure-3.11

When the MATLAB program in Figure-3.11 is run we get an output as in Figure-3.12.

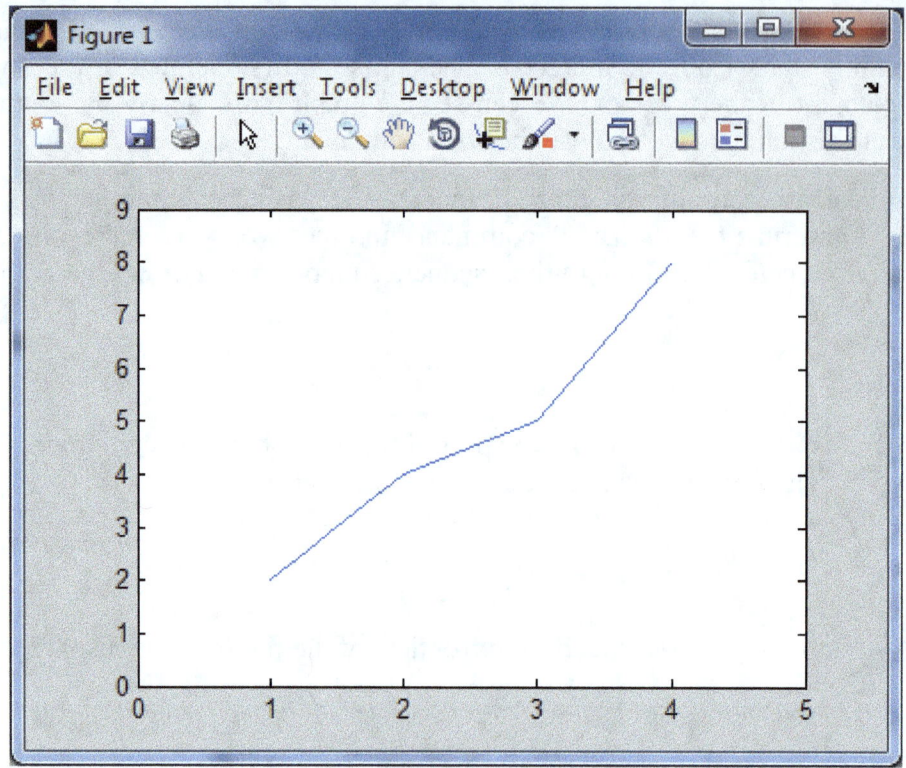

Figure-3.12

Example-3.5:

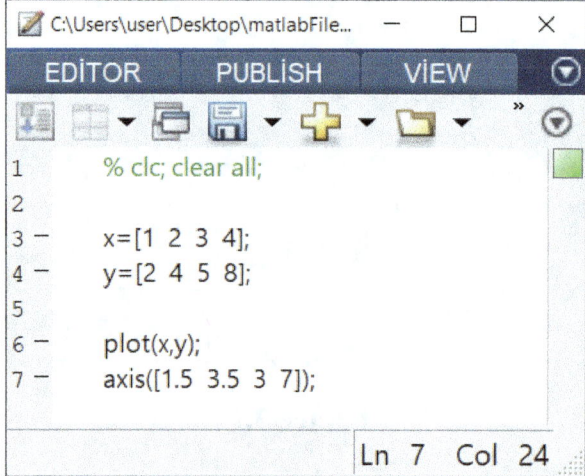

Figure-3.13

When the MATLAB program in Figure-3.13 is run we get an output as in Figure-3.14.

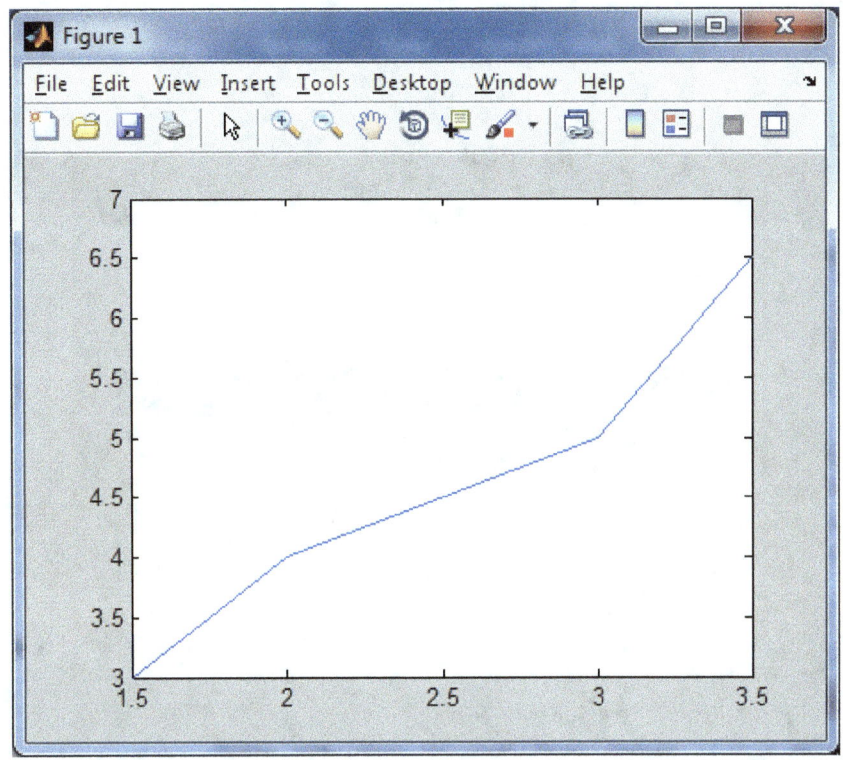

Figure-3.14

3.4 Determination of Coordinates

The general use of the plot() function is as

$$\text{plot}(x, y, \text{'s'})$$

where 's' determines the properties of the drawn graph, and it consists of at most three letters and at least one letter. If the coordinate points are to be shown explicitly, then we can use one of the symbols in Table-3.1 for the 's' parameter.

Table-3.1 The symbols used for marking of the coordinate points.

o	circle
x	x-mark
+	plus
*	star
s	square
d	diamond
v	triangle
^	triangle

<   triangle

>   triangle

p   pentagram

h   hexagram

Example-3.6:

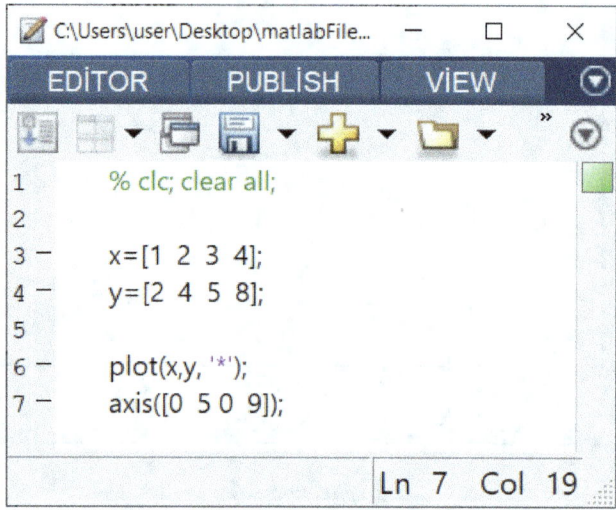

Figure-3.15

When the MATLAB program in Figure-3.15 is run we get an output as in Figure-3.16.

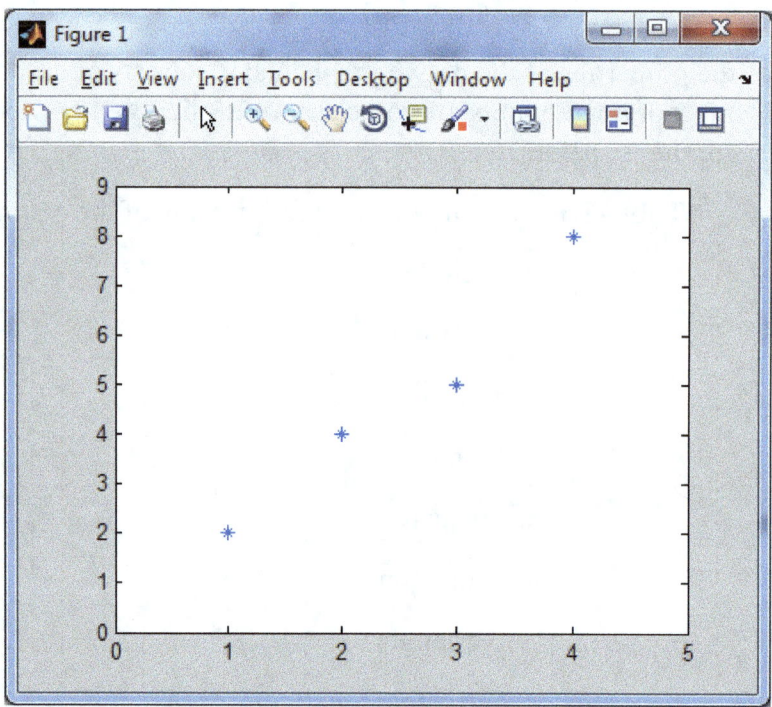

Figure-3.16

If the lines which are used to connect the coordinates have specific properties, then the 's' parameter in plot(x, y, 's') consists of two characters. The first character is chosen from Table-3.1 and the second character is taken from Table-3.2.

Table-3.2 Line types

-     solid
:   dotted
-.   dashdot
--   dashed

Example-3.7:

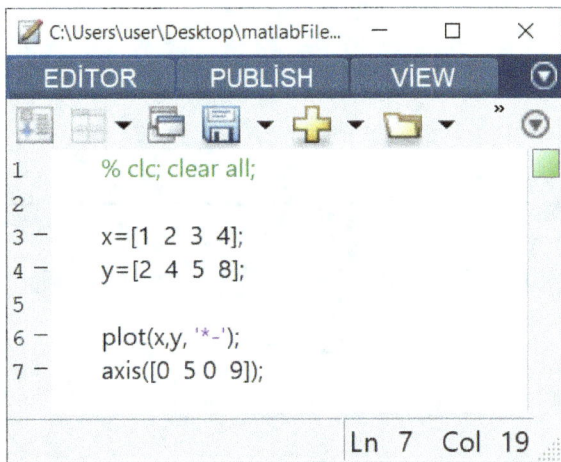

Figure-3.17

When the MATLAB program in Figure-3.17 is run we get an output as in Figure-3.18.

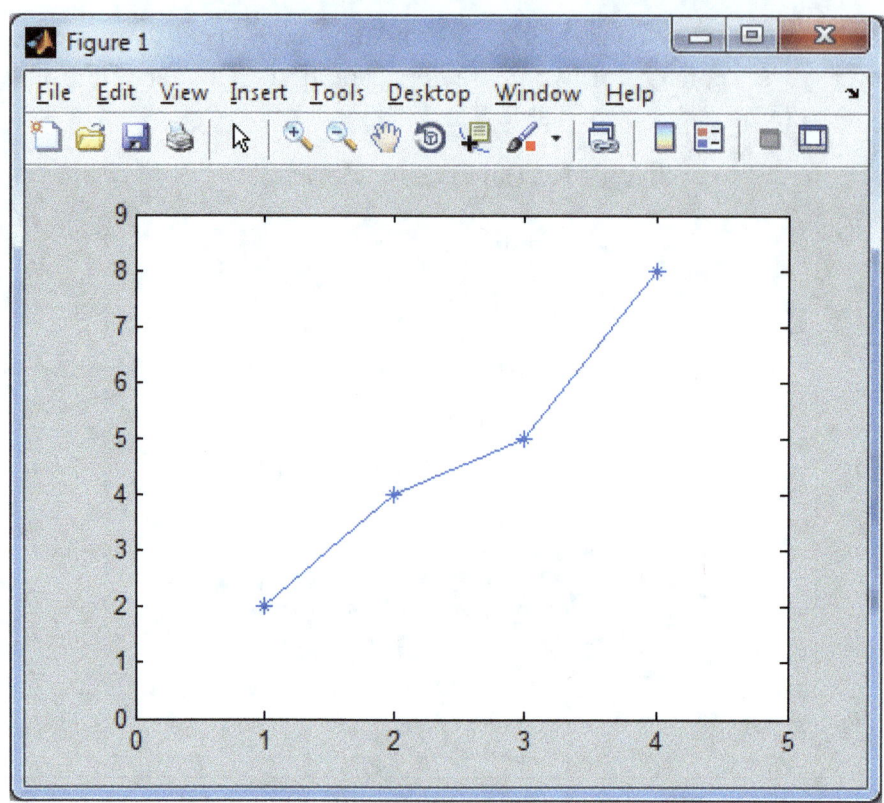

Figure-3.18

Example-3.8:

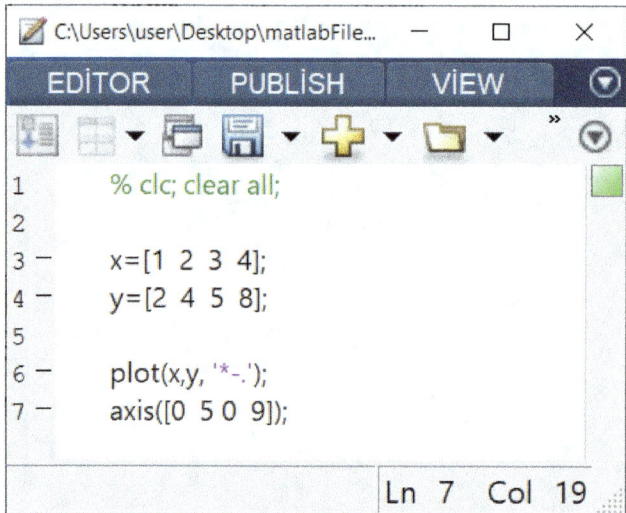

Figure-3.19

When the MATLAB program in Figure-3.19 is run we get an output as in Figure-3.20

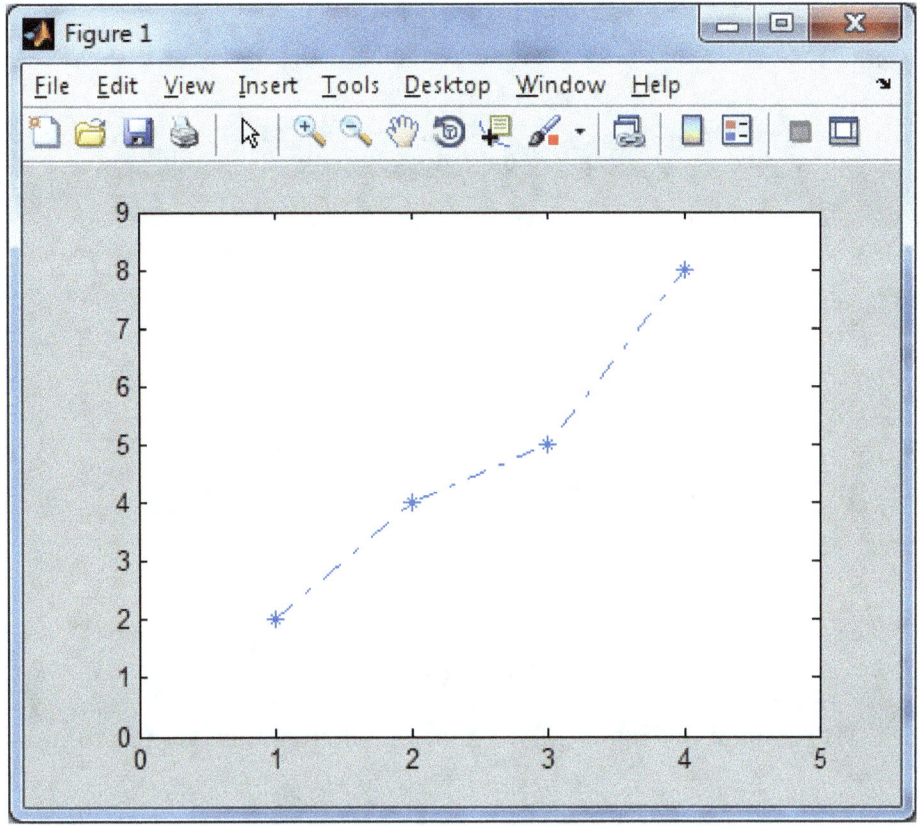

Figure-3.20

If we want the lines to be drawn to be colored, a third character is added to the 's' variable in the plot(x, y, 's') command. The third character is selected from Table-3.3.

Tabl3-3.3 Color parameters

b	blue
g	green
r	red
c	cyan
m	magenta
y	yellow
k	black
w	white

Example-3.9:

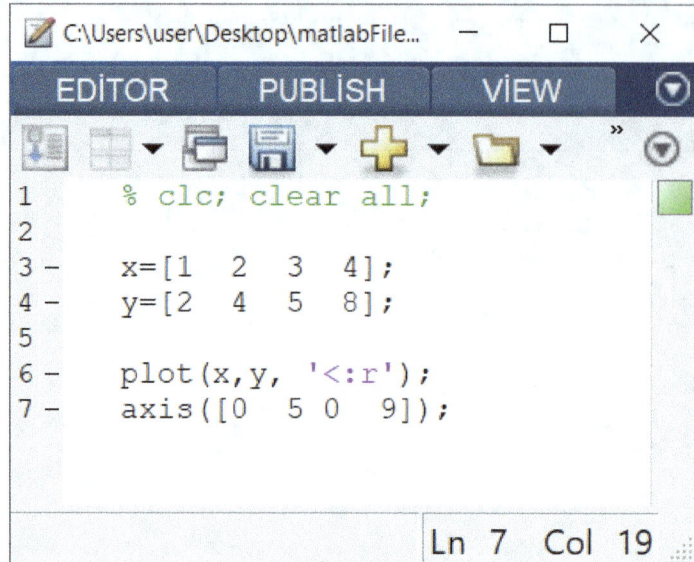

Figure-3.21

When the MATLAB program in Figure-3.21 is run we get an output as in Figure-3.22.

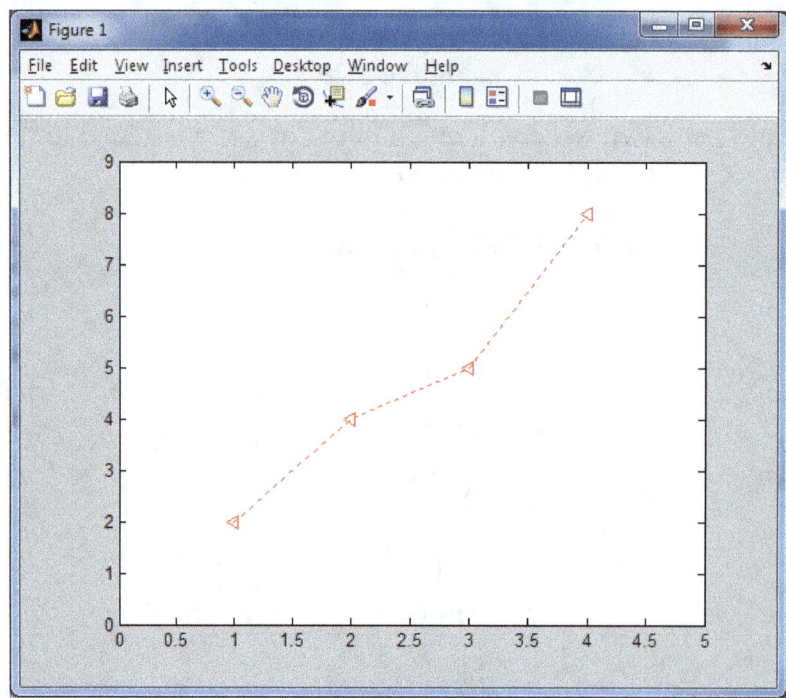

Figure-3.22

A single graph is drawn on Figure-3.22. More than one graph can be drawn on the same figure using the "HOLD ON" command.

3.5 HOLD ON Command

The HOLD ON command is used to keep more than one graphic on the same figure. If HOLD ON is not used, the last graphic drawn remains on the figure.

Example-3.10:

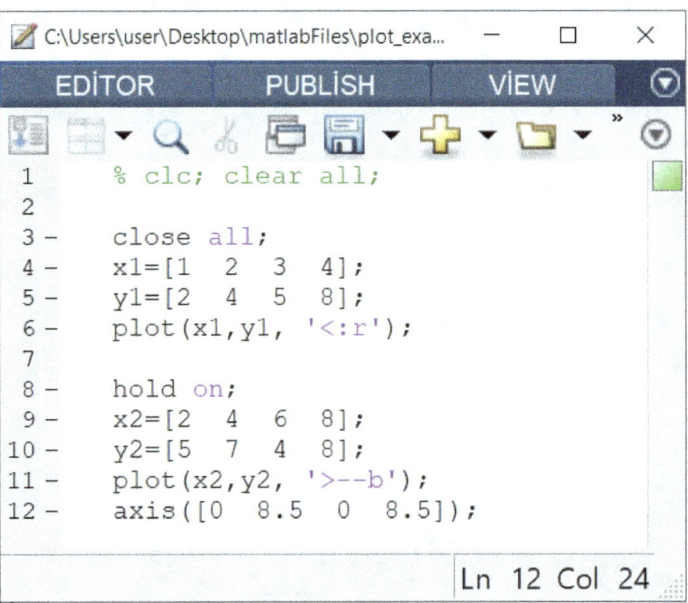

Figure-3.23

When the MATLAB program in Figure-3.23 is run we get an output as in Figure-3.24.

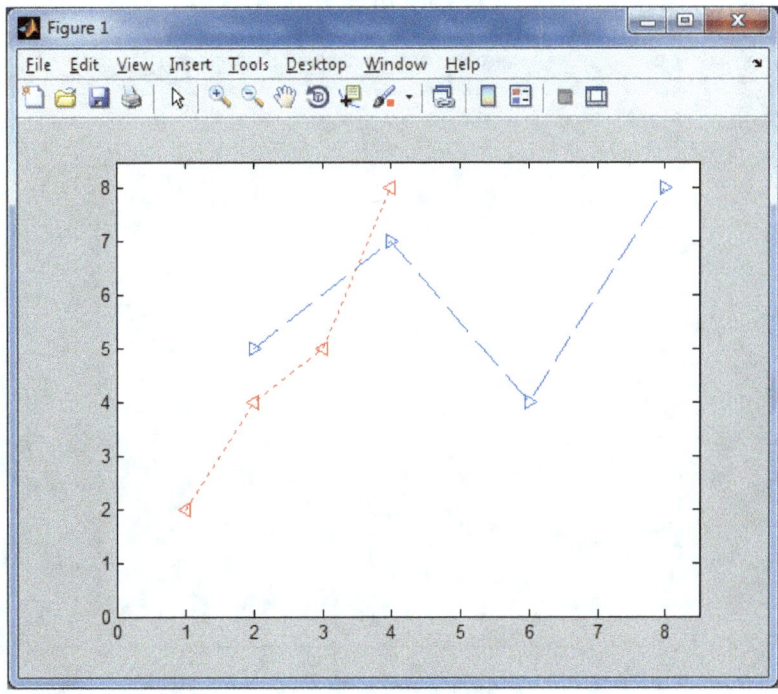

Figure-3.24

It is enough to write the HOLD ON command once to keep all graphics on the same figure. The HOLD ON command should be written after the "*plot*" command.

Example-3.11:

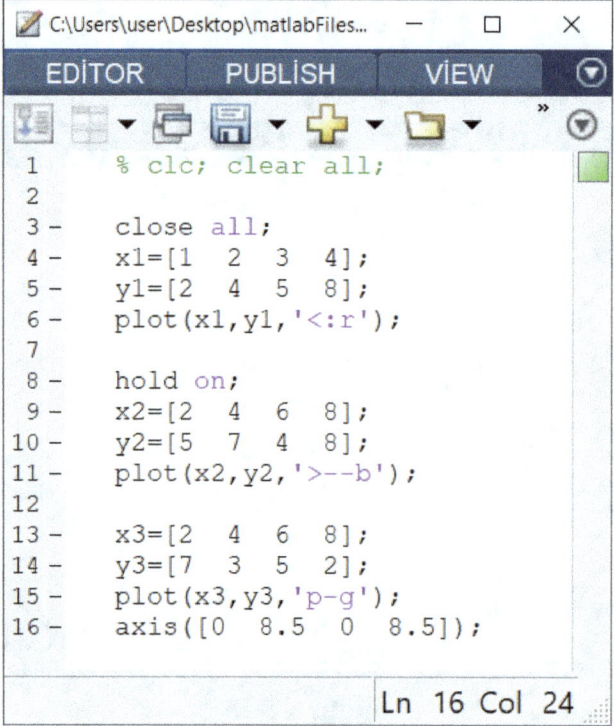

Figure-3.25

The output of the program in Figure-3.25 is shown in Figure-3.26.

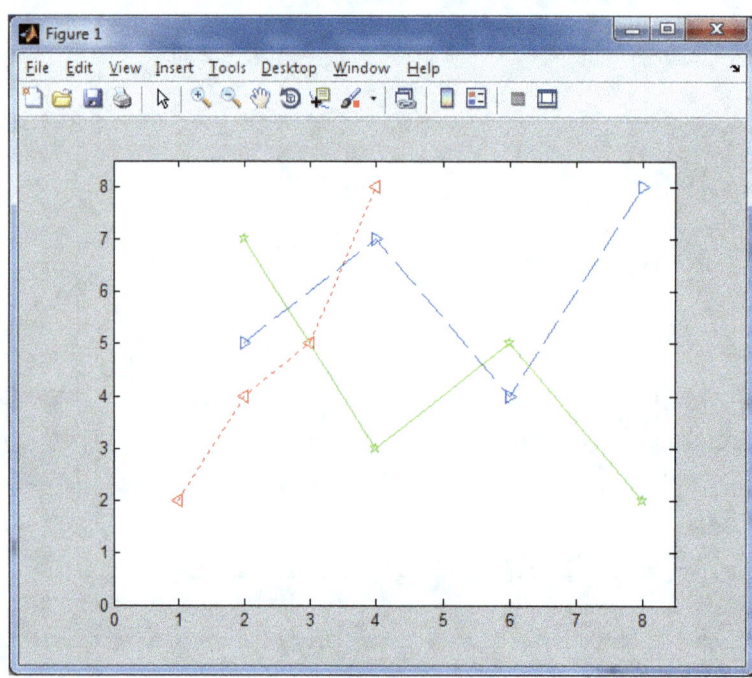

Figure-3.26

3.6 HOLD OFF Command

Once the HOLD ON command is typed, all drawn graphics stay on the figure. HOLD OFF command is used to cancel the HOLD ON command.

Example-3.12:

C:\Users\user\Desktop\matlab...

EDİT... PUBL... VİEW

```
% clc; clear all;

close all;
x1=[1  2  3  4];
y1=[2  4  5  8];
plot(x1,y1,'<:r');

hold on;
x2=[2  4  6  8];
y2=[5  7  4  8];
plot(x2,y2,'>--b');

hold off;
x3=[2  4  6  8];
y3=[7  3  5  2];
plot(x3,y3,'p-g');
axis([0  8.5  0  8.5]);
```

Ln 17 Col 24

Figure-3.27

When the MATLAB program in Figure-3.27 is executed we get the graph in Figure-3.28.

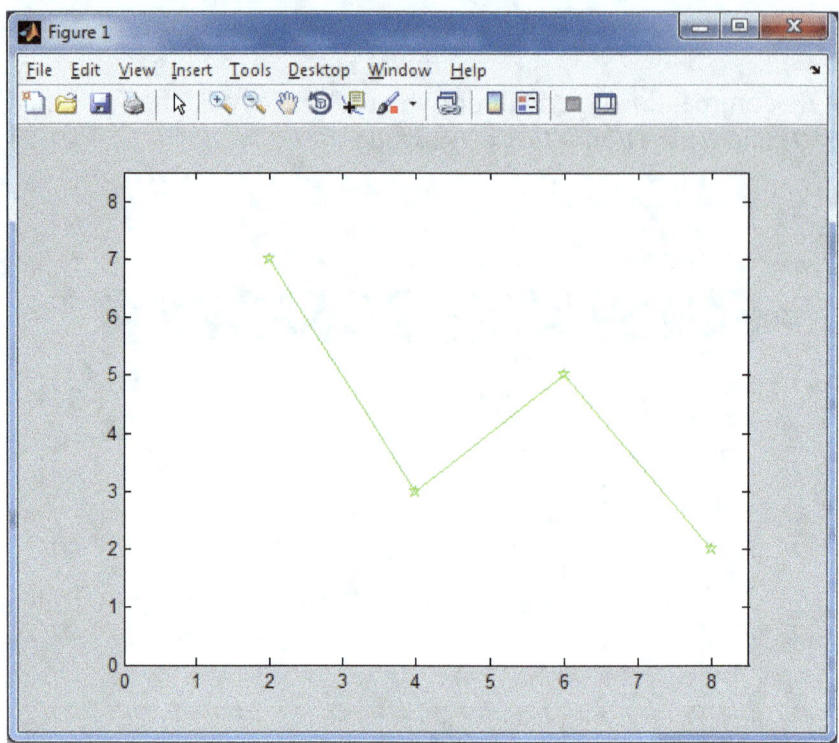

Figure-3.28

"XLABEL", "YLABEL", and "TITLE" commands are used to put labels on the horizontal axis, vertical axis and the top of the figure.

3.7 XLABEL, YLABEL, and TITLE Commands

XLABEL is used as

$$\texttt{xlabel('Label Text')}$$

If the label on the x axis is to be colored, bolded, etc, then we use the XLABEL command as

$$\texttt{xlabel('Label Text', 'property1', 'property2',...)}$$

YLABEL is used as

$$\texttt{ylabel('Label Text')}$$

If the label on the y axis is to be colored, bolded, etc, then we use the YLABEL command as

$$\texttt{ylabel('Label Text', 'property1', 'property2',...)}$$

TITLE is used as

$$\texttt{title('Label Text')}$$

If the label on the title is to be colored, bolded, etc, then we use the TITLE command as

```
title('Label Text', 'property1', 'property2',...)
```

Example-3.13:

```
% clc; clear all;

close all;
x1=[1  2  3  4];
y1=[2  4  5  8];
plot(x1,y1,'<:r');

hold on;
x2=[2  4  6  8];
y2=[5  7  4  8];
plot(x2,y2,'>--b');

%hold off;
x3=[2  4  6  8];
y3=[7  3  5  2];
plot(x3,y3,'p-g');
axis([0  8.5  0  8.5]);

title('Example');
xlabel('Time Axis');
ylabel('Function Values');
```

Figure-3.29

When the MATLAB program in Figure-3.29 is executed, we get the graph in Figure-3.30.

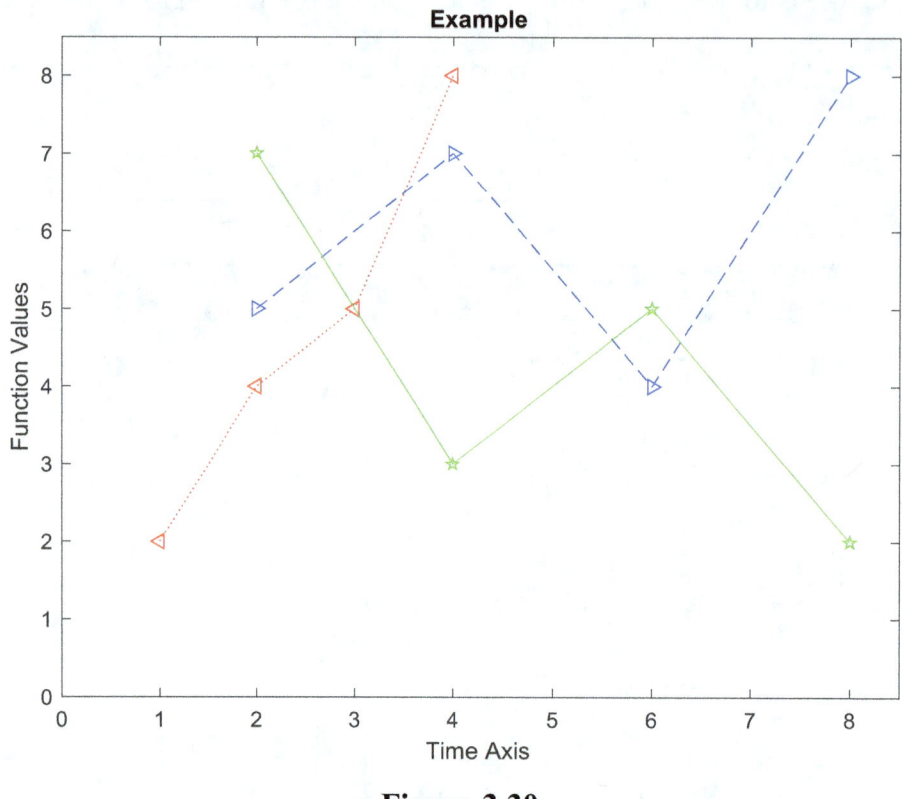

Figure-3.30

Subscript and superscript characters can be used with XLABEL, YLABEL and TITLE commands, and for subscript '_' and for superscript '^' is used.

Example-3.14:

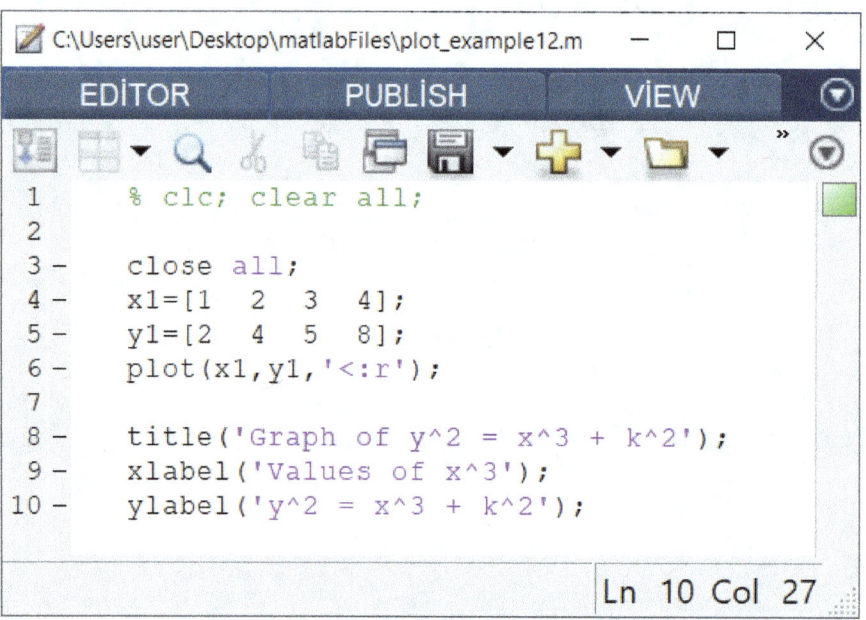

Figure-3.31

When the MATLAB program in Figure-3.31 is executed, we get the graph in Figure-3.32.

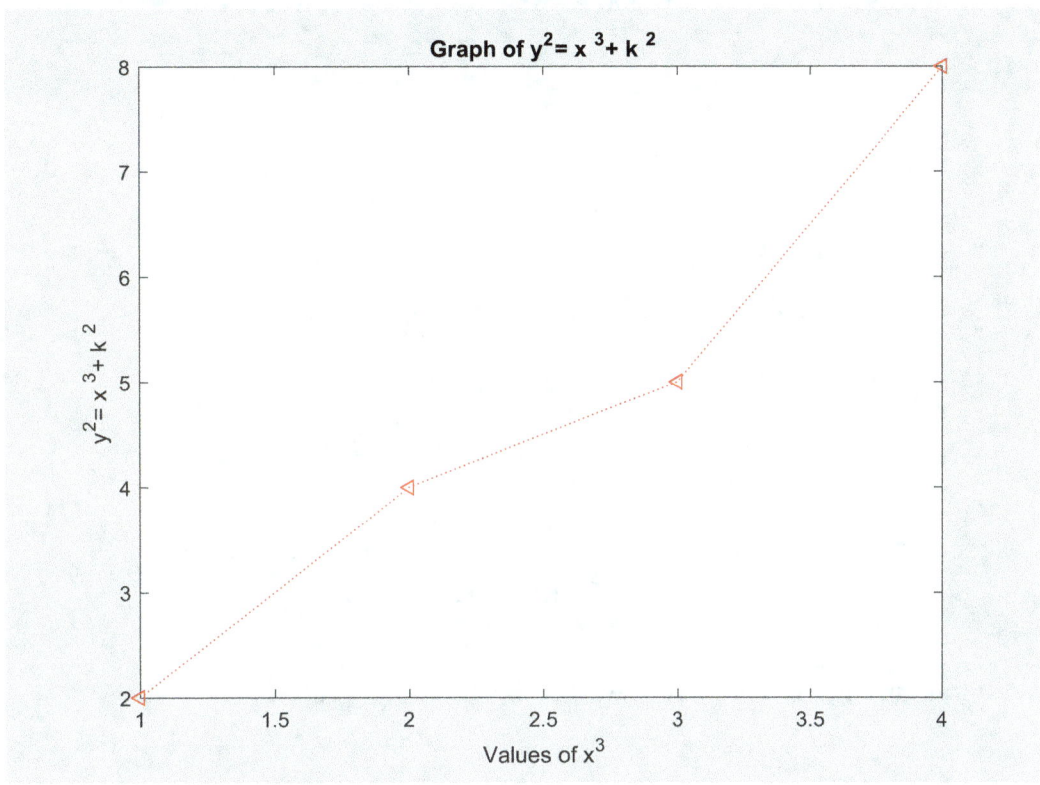

Figure-3.32

3.8 GTEXT Command

This command used to add "text" with the mouse to any part of the graph drawn with the PLOT command. It is used as

$$\textbf{gtext}(\text{'Any Text'})$$

Example-3.15:

```
C:\Users\user\Desktop\matlabFiles\plot_example12.m

    EDITOR          PUBLISH          VIEW

1       % clc; clear all;
2
3 -     close all;
4 -     x1=[1   2   3   4];
5 -     y1=[2   4   5   8];
6 -     plot(x1,y1,'<:r');
7
8 -     title('Example for gtext');
9 -     xlabel('Time Axis');
10-     ylabel('Function Values');
11
12-     gtext('Place any text on the graph');

script                                    Ln 12 Col 38
```

Figure-3.33

When the program in Figure-3.33 is run, we get the graph in Figure-3.34.

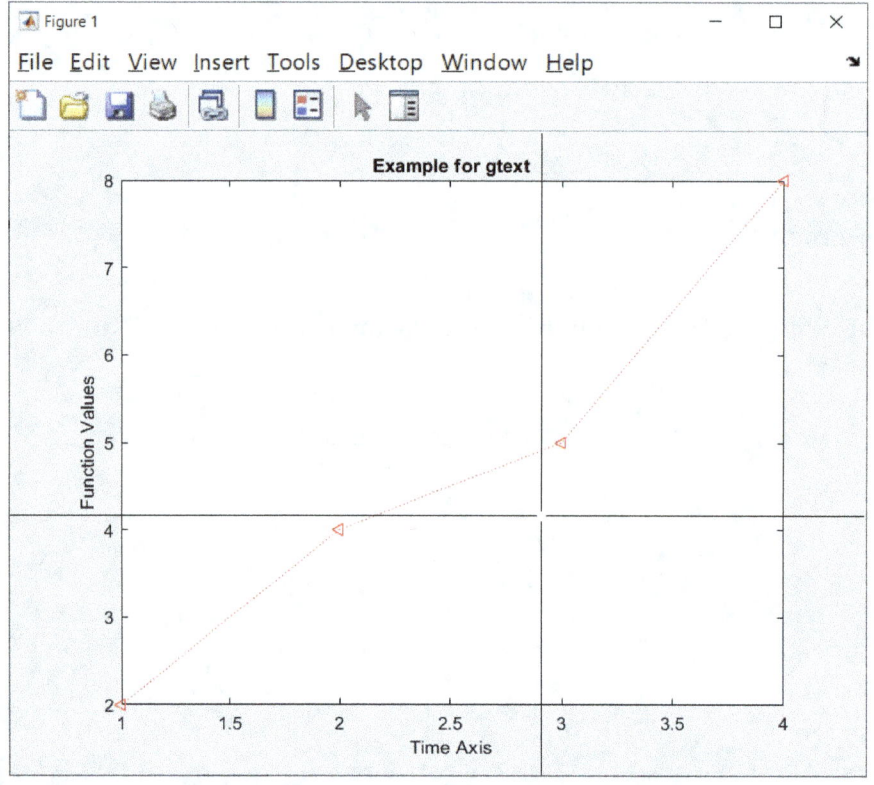

Figure-3.34

When we click the mouse, the text in the gtext(···) command is placed to the screen and the place lies to the right of the midpoint of the plus sign. In other words, when the mouse is pressed, the graph looks like as in Figure-3.35.

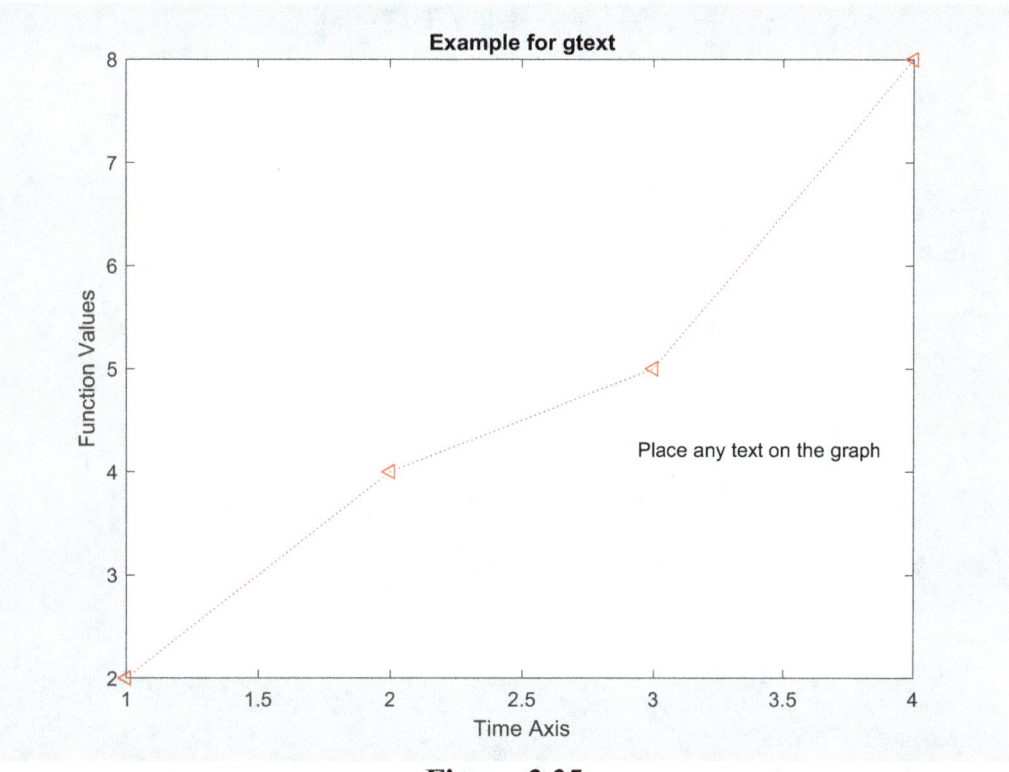

Figure-3.35

3.9 LEGEND Command

LEGEND command is used to give brief information the graphics on the figure. The information provided appears in the upper right corner of the figure. Its use is as

```
legend('first graph explanation','second graph explanation',...)
```

3.10 GRIN ON Command

GRIN ON command is used to place grid lines on the drawn graph. It may become easier to read some values on the graph with the help of grid lines. We can disable the GRIN ON command by typing GRID OFF.

Example-3.16:

```matlab
% clc; clear all;

close all;
x1=[1  2  3  4];
y1=[2  4  5  8];
plot(x1,y1,'<:r');

hold on;
x2=[2  4  6  8];
y2=[5  7  4  8];
plot(x2,y2,'>--b');

x3=[2  4  6  8];
y3=[7  3  5  2];
plot(x3,y3,'p-g');
axis([0  8.5  0  8.5]);

title('Example');
xlabel('Time Axis');
ylabel('Function Values');
legend('First Graph', 'Second Graph', 'Third Graph');
grid on;
```

Figure-3.36

When the program in Figure-3.36 is run, we get the graph in Figure-3.37.

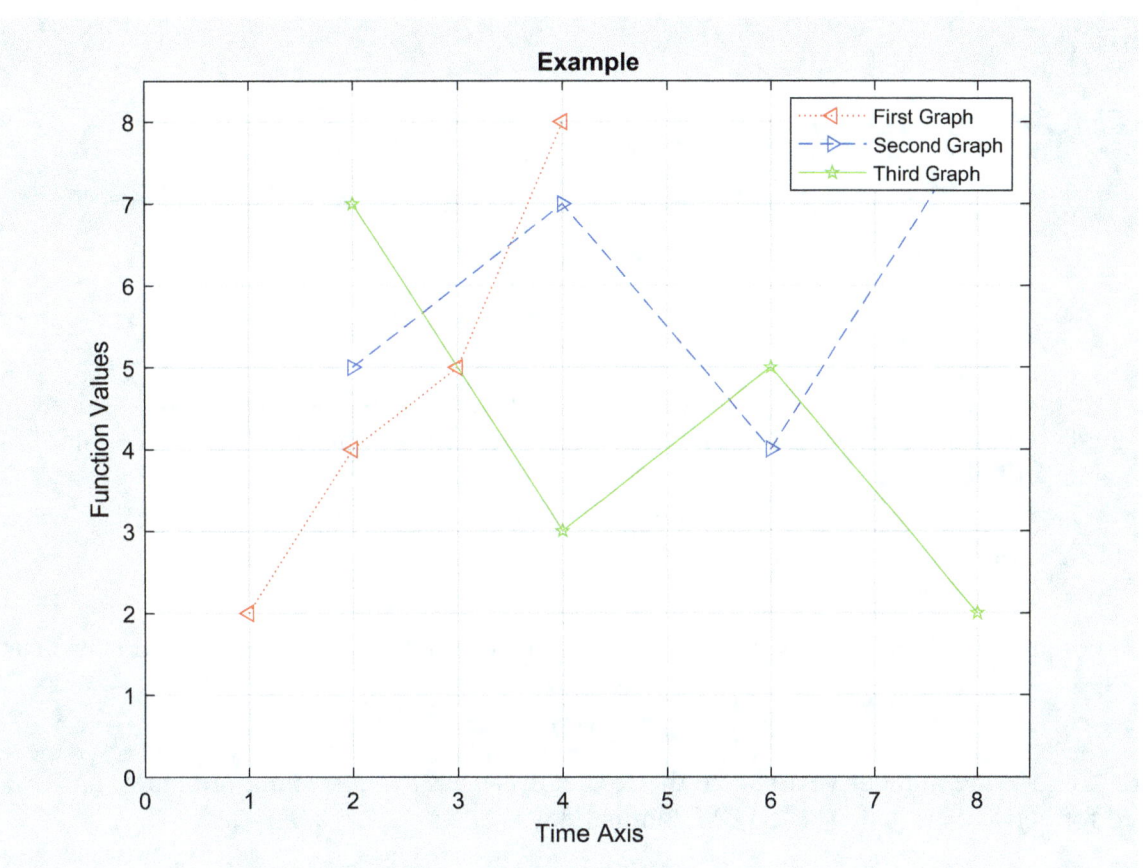

Figure-3.37

Chapter-4

MATLAB Commands-4

Abstract: In this chapter we will first discuss in details the "stem" command used to draw graphs of digital signals. Later, explanations and examples containing the "subplot" and "figure" commands will be given.

4.1 STEM Command

STEM command is used to draw discrete time signals or functions. This command is used as

$$\texttt{stem(X,Y)}$$

where X and Y are number vectors and the X vector is used for horizontal ordinates, and Y vector is used for vertical ordinates. If STEM command is used as

$$\texttt{stem(Y)}$$

then the elements of the Y vector are placed to the vertical axis according to their index values, i.e., X vector consists of the indices of the Y elements.

The symbols used to select color, line type, and coordinate marks for the PLOT command can also be used for the STEM command. Apart from this, XLABEL, YLABEL, TITLE, and AXIS commands can also be used with the STEM command.

In other words, all graphic parameters used with the PLOT command can also be used with the STEM command.

Example-4.1:

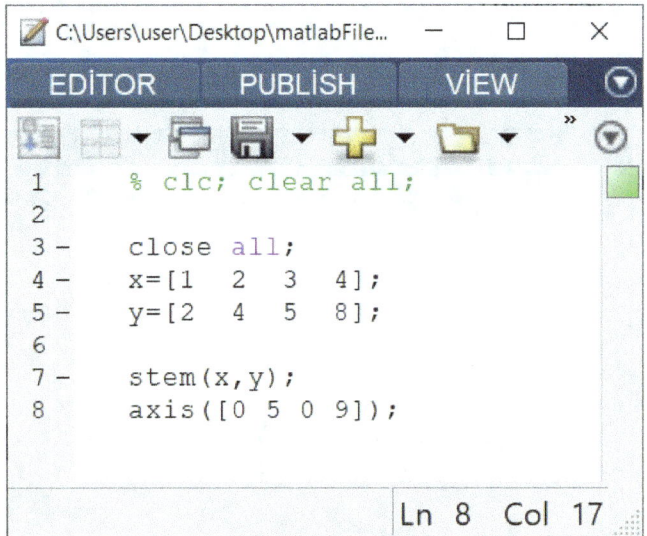

Figure-4.1

When the program in Figure-4.1 is run, we get the graph in Figure-4.2.

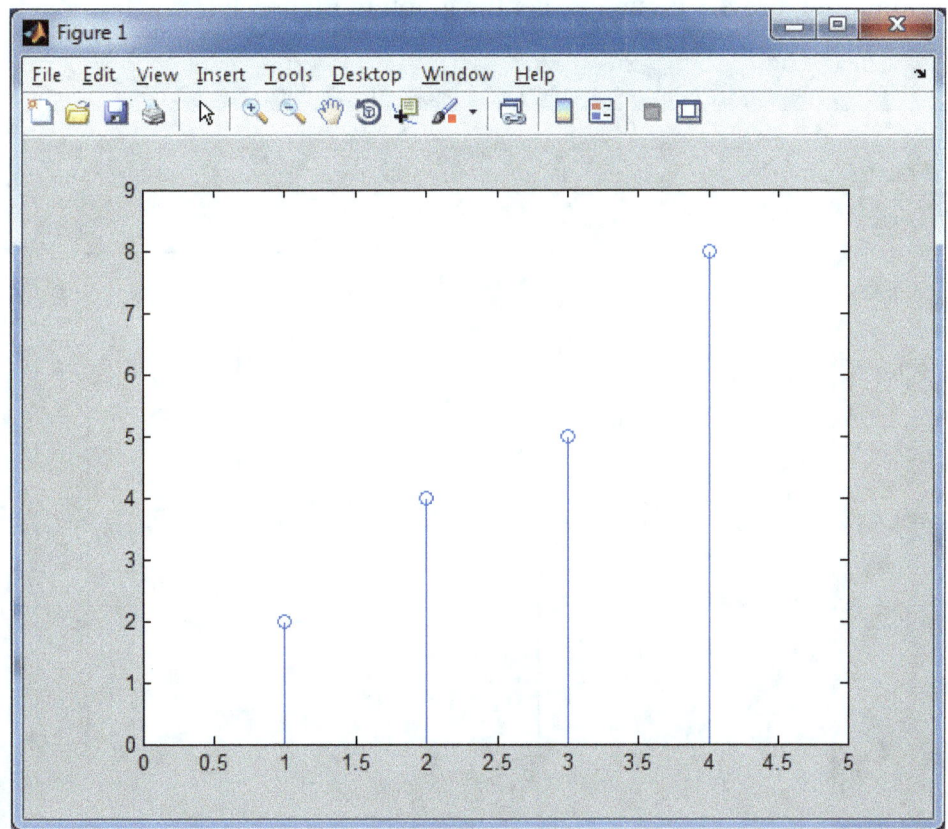

Figure-4.2

If the coordinate points are to be filled with small circles, then use the STEM command is used as

`stem(X, Y,'filled')`

Example-4.2:

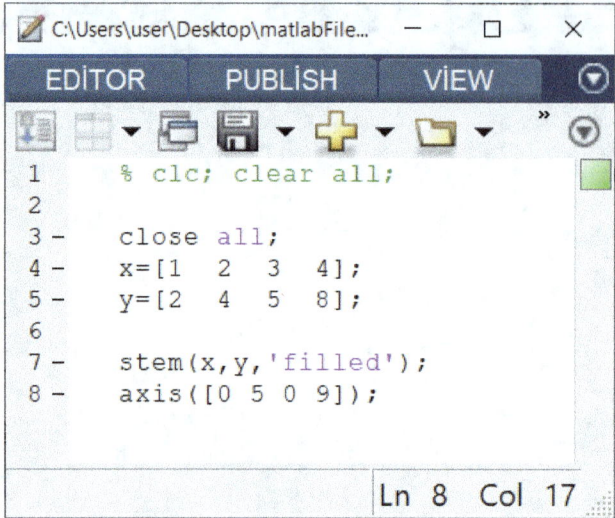

Figure-4.3

When the program in Figure-4.3 is run, we get the graph in Figure-4.4.

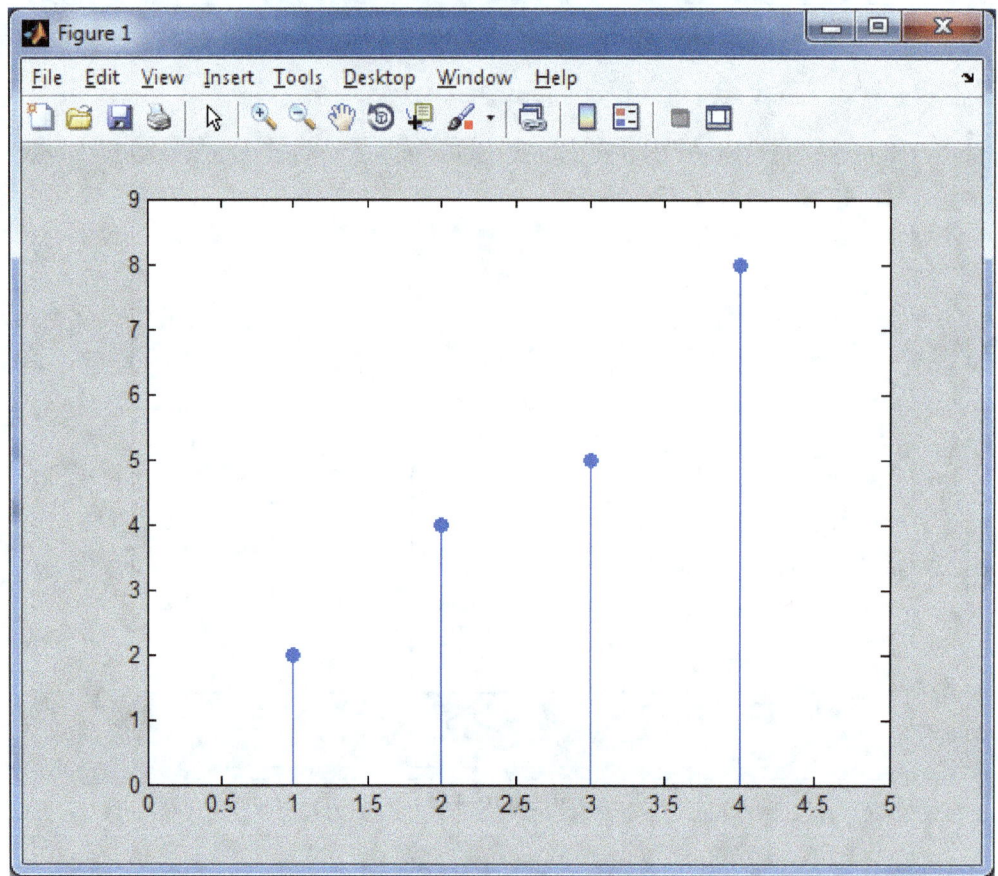

Figure-4.4

The most general use of the stem command is as

```
stem(X, Y,'filled', LINE SPECS) or stem(X, Y, LINE SPECS, 'filled')
```

Example-4.3:

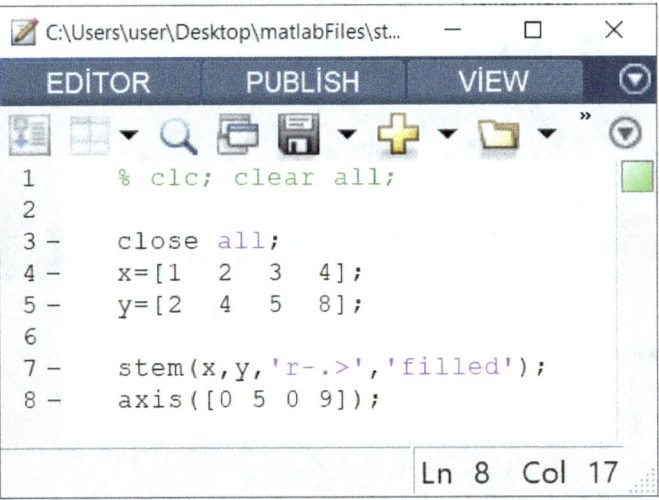

Figure-4.5

When the program in Figure-4.5 is run, we get the graph in Figure-4.6.

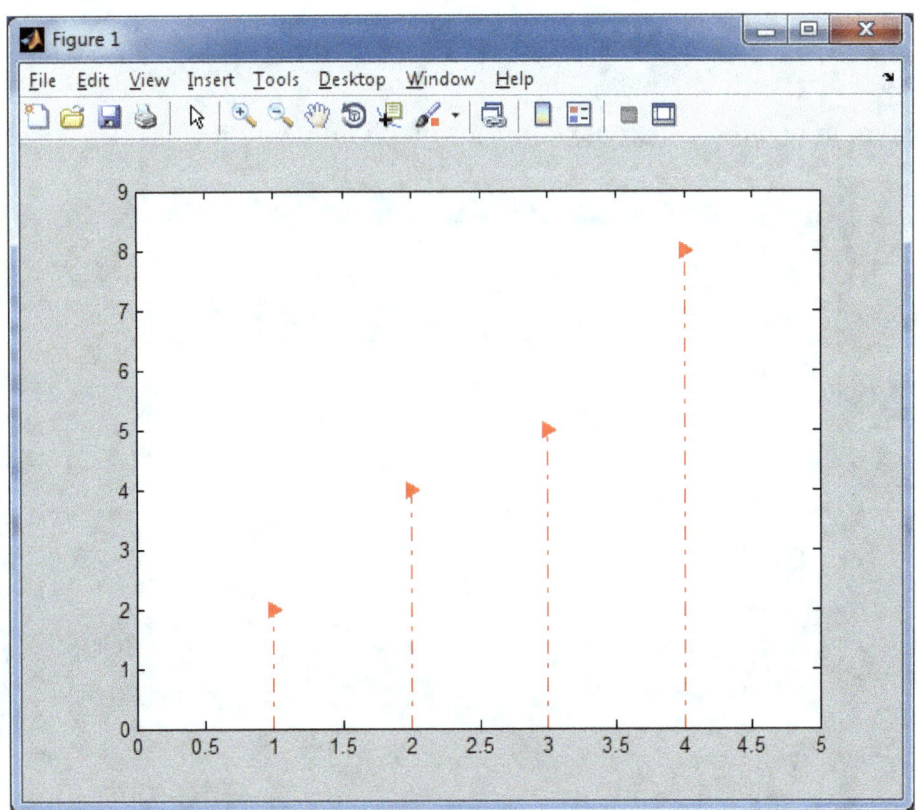

Figure-4.6

To change the interior color of the shapes at the top of the vertical lines, we can use the STEM command as

stem(X, Y,'filled', LINE SPECS, 'MarkerFaceColor', 'x')

where 'x' indicates the interior color.

Example-4.4:

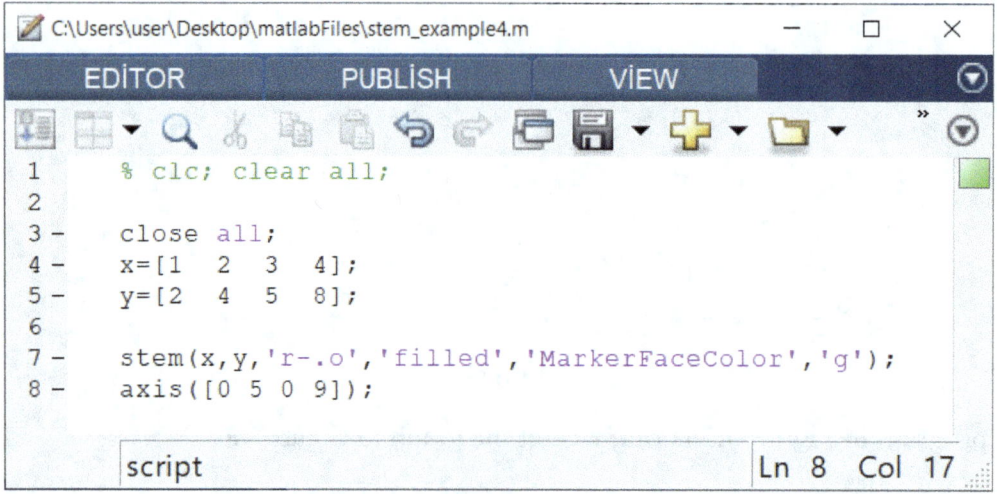

Figure-4.7

When the program in Figure-4.7 is run, we get the graph in Figure-4.8.

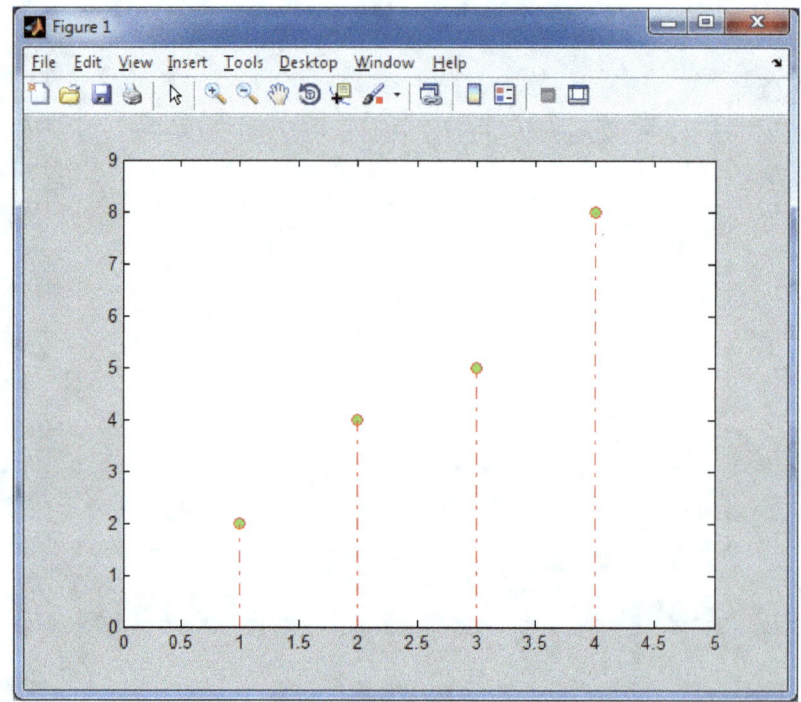

Figure-4.8

To change the frontier color of the shapes at the top of the vertical lines, we can use the STEM command as

```
stem(X,Y,'filled',LINE SPECS,'MarkerFaceColor','x','MarkerEdgeColor', 'y')
```

where 'y' is the color parameter for the frontier.

Example-4.5:

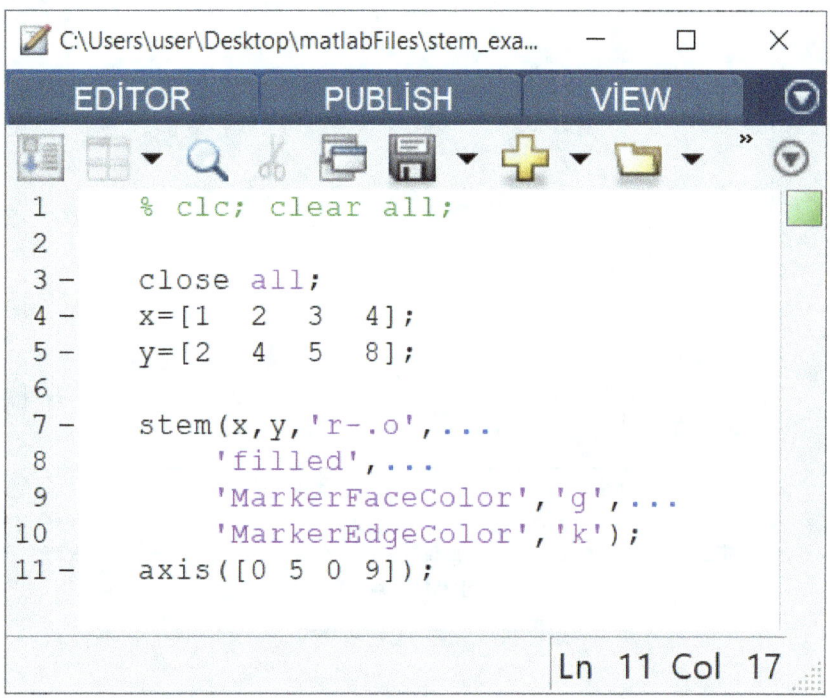

Figure-4.9

When the program in Figure-4.9 is run, we get the graph in Figure-4.10.

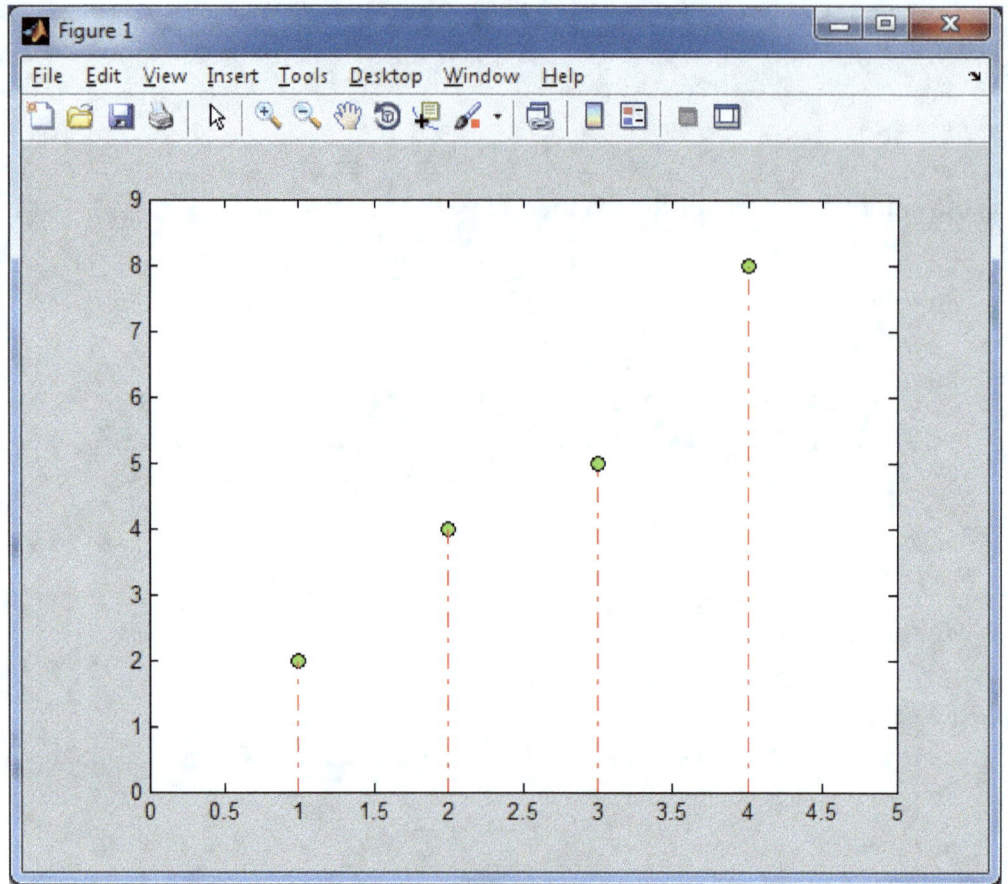

Figure-4.10

Note: For MATLAB commands that cannot fit to a single line, we can use '...' at the end of the line to break the MATLAB command into two lines, in the previous example we used this feature.

It is possible to draw more than one graphic on the same figure with the STEM Command. In this case, the command is used as

$$\texttt{stem(X,Y)}$$

where if X is a vector and Y is a matrix such that Y=[Y_1 Y_2 $\cdots$] where Y_1 Y_2 $\cdots$ are the columns of the matrix.

In this case each column of Y is drawn with the same X vector. If X is a matrix such that X=[X_1 X_2 $\cdots$] and Y=[Y_1 Y_2 $\cdots$], in this case, a column of Y is matched with a column of X such that they have the same column index and the matched pair is drawn.

Example-4.6:

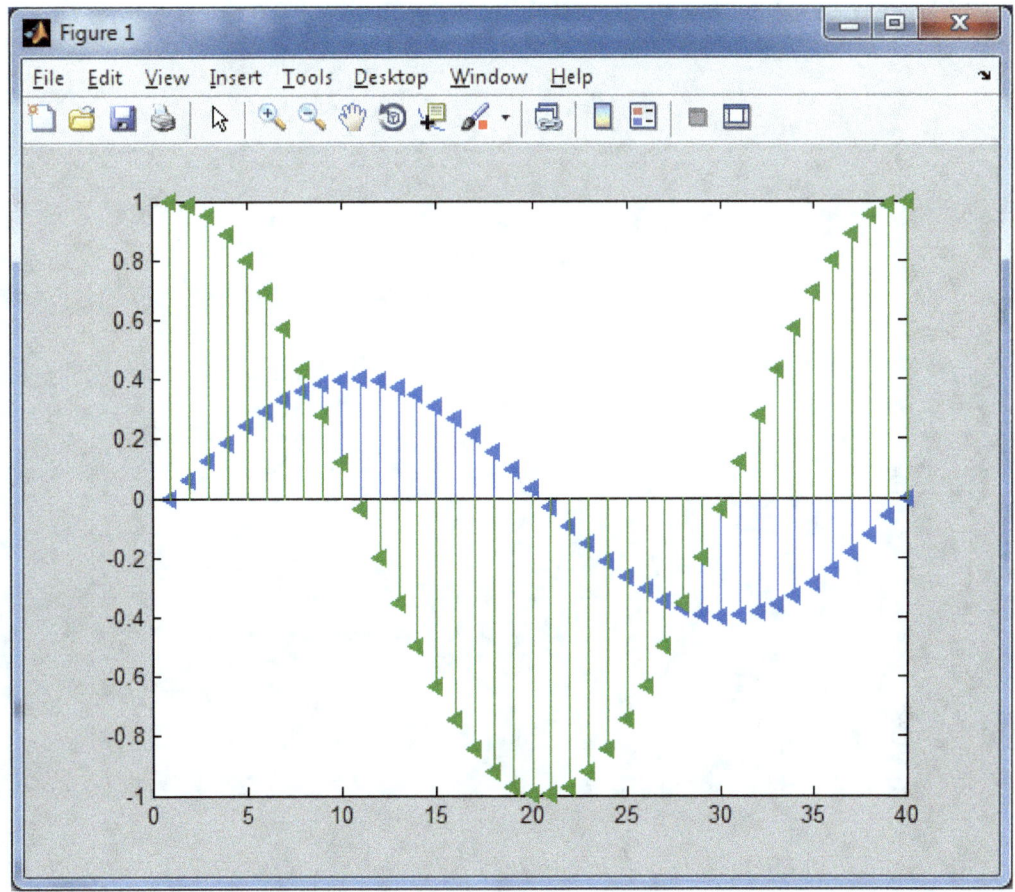

Figure-4.11

When the program in Figure-4.11 is run, we get the graph in Figure-4.12.

Figure-4.12

Example-4.7:

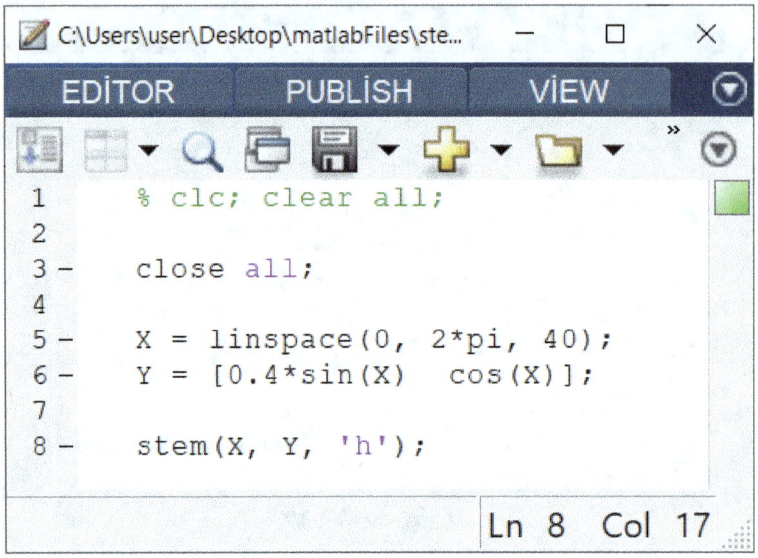
C:\Users\user\Desktop\matlabFiles\ste...
EDİTOR
PUBLİSH
VİEW
% clc; clear all;
close all;
X = linspace(0, 2*pi, 40);
Y = [0.4*sin(X)   cos(X)];
stem(X, Y, 'h');
Ln 8
Col 17

Figure-4.13

When the program in Figure-4.13 is run, we get the graph in Figure-4.14

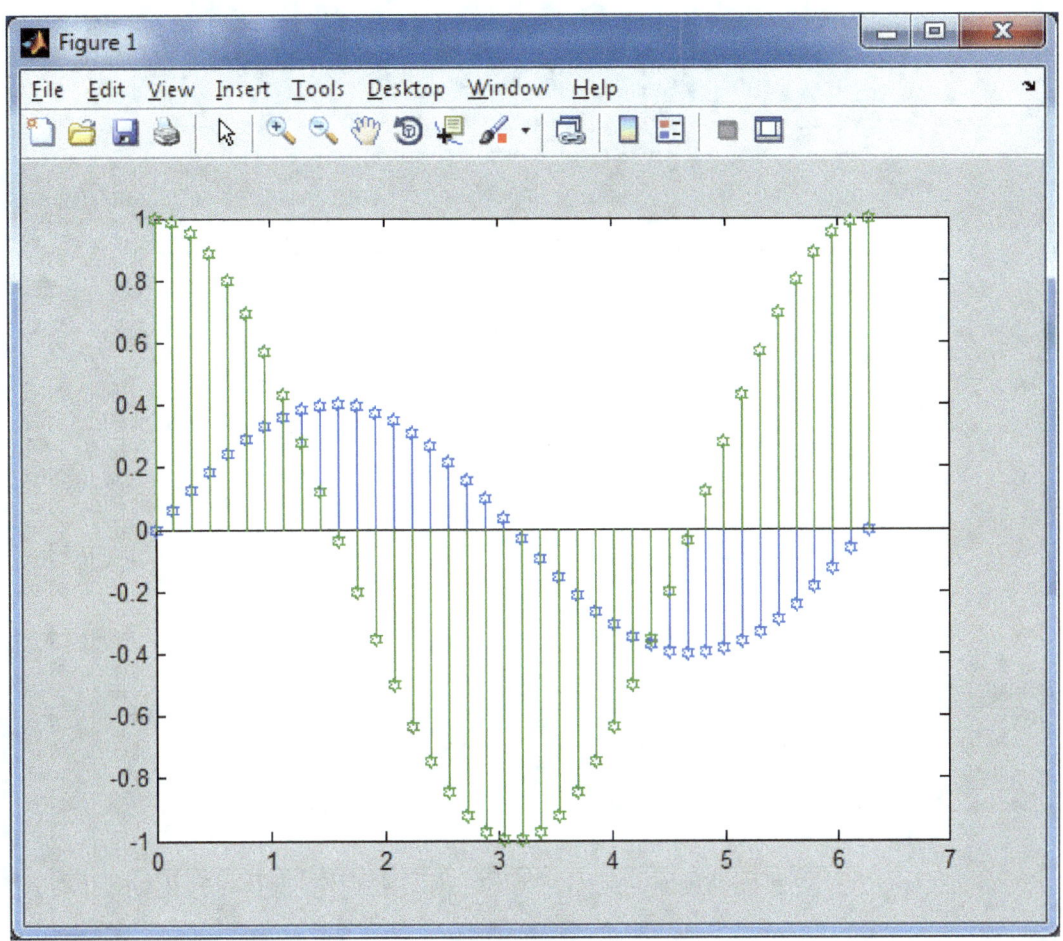

Figure-4.14

Example-4.8:

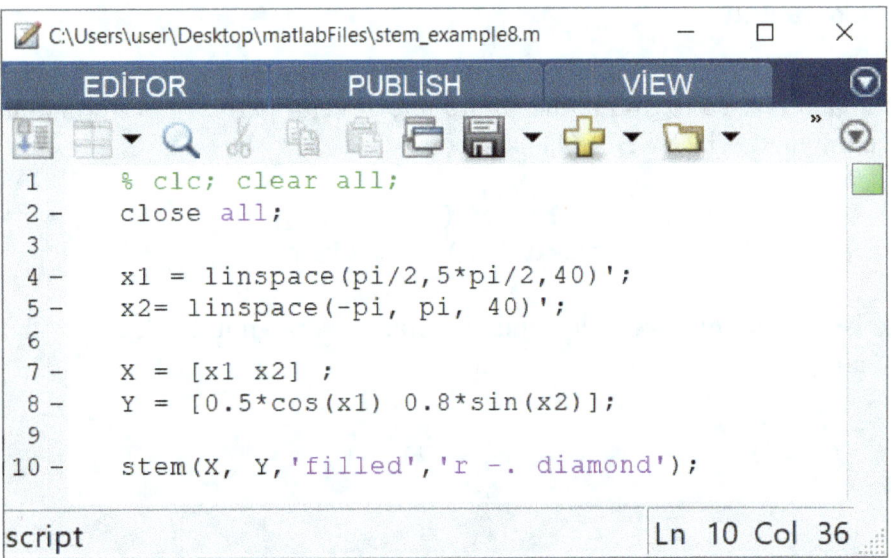

Figure-4.15

When the program in Figure-4.15 is run, we get the graph in Figure-4.16

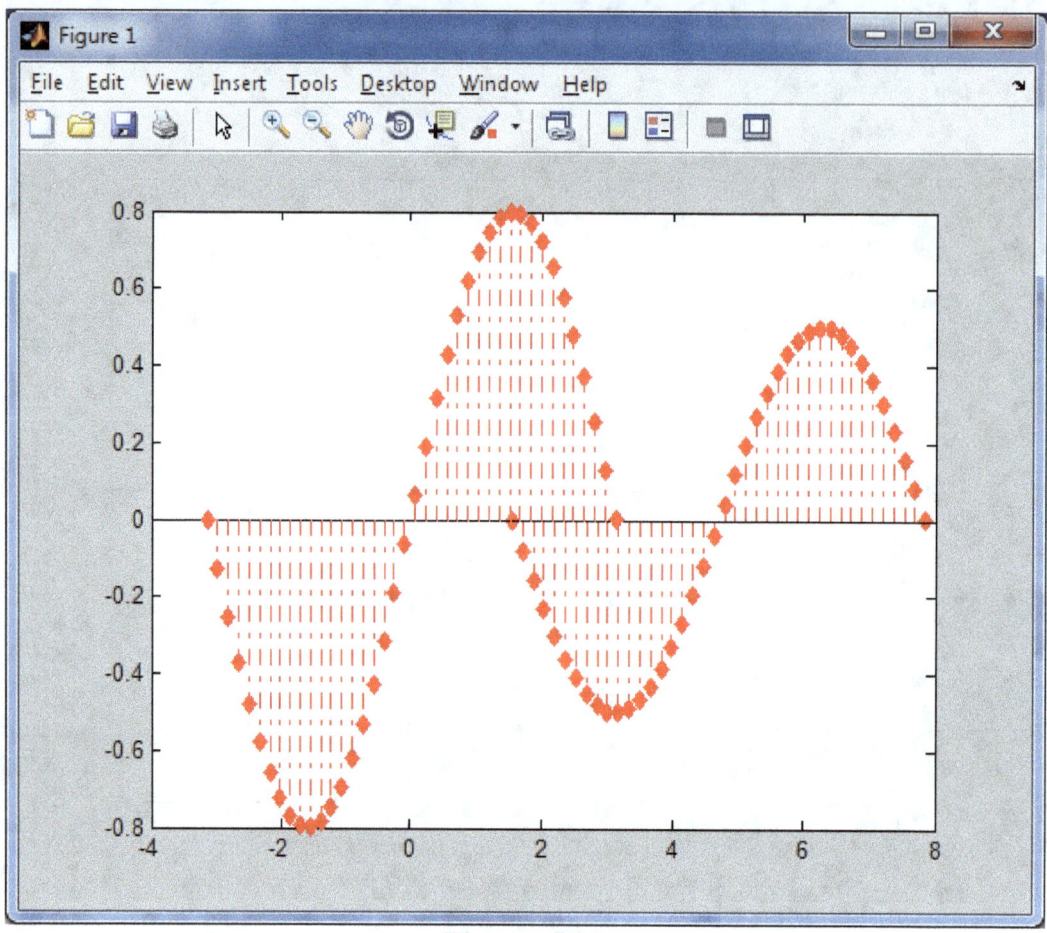

Figure-4.16

4.2 SUBPLOT Command

SUBPLOT command is used to divide the figure into several parts. PLOT command is used after the SUBPLOT command. The SUBPLOT is used as

```
subplot(m,n,k)
plot(..) or stem(..)
```

Here, the figure is divided into mxn cells and any graph is drawn in the k cell with the next PLOT or STEM command.

Example-4.9:

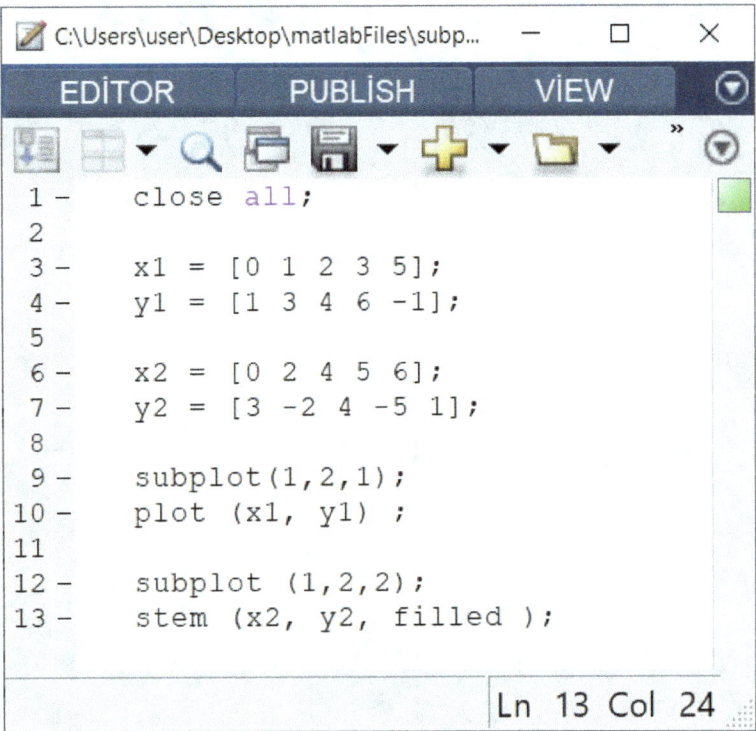

Figure-4.17

When the program in Figure-4.17 is run, we get the graph in Figure-4.18

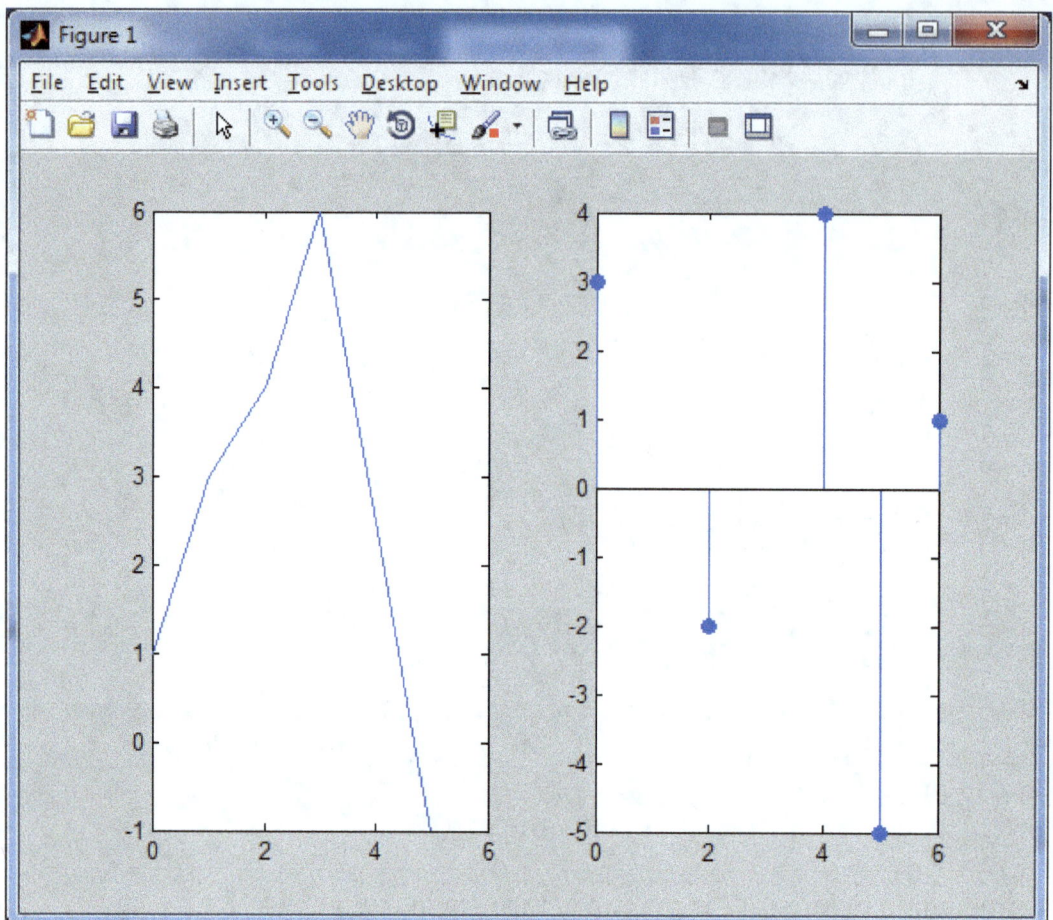

Figure-4.18

Example-4.10:

```
clc; clear all;
close all;

t = linspace(0,2,100);

f = 1;
y1 = sin(2*pi*f*t);
subplot(2,2,1);
plot(t, y1);


f = 2;
y2 = sin(2*pi*f*t);
subplot(2,2,2);
plot(t,y2);

f = 4;
y3 = sin(2*pi*f*t);
subplot(2,2,3);
plot(t,y3);

f = 8;
y4 = sin(2*pi*f*t);
subplot(2,2,4);
plot(t, y4);
```

Figure-4.19

When the program in Figure-4.19 is run, we get the graph in Figure-4.20.

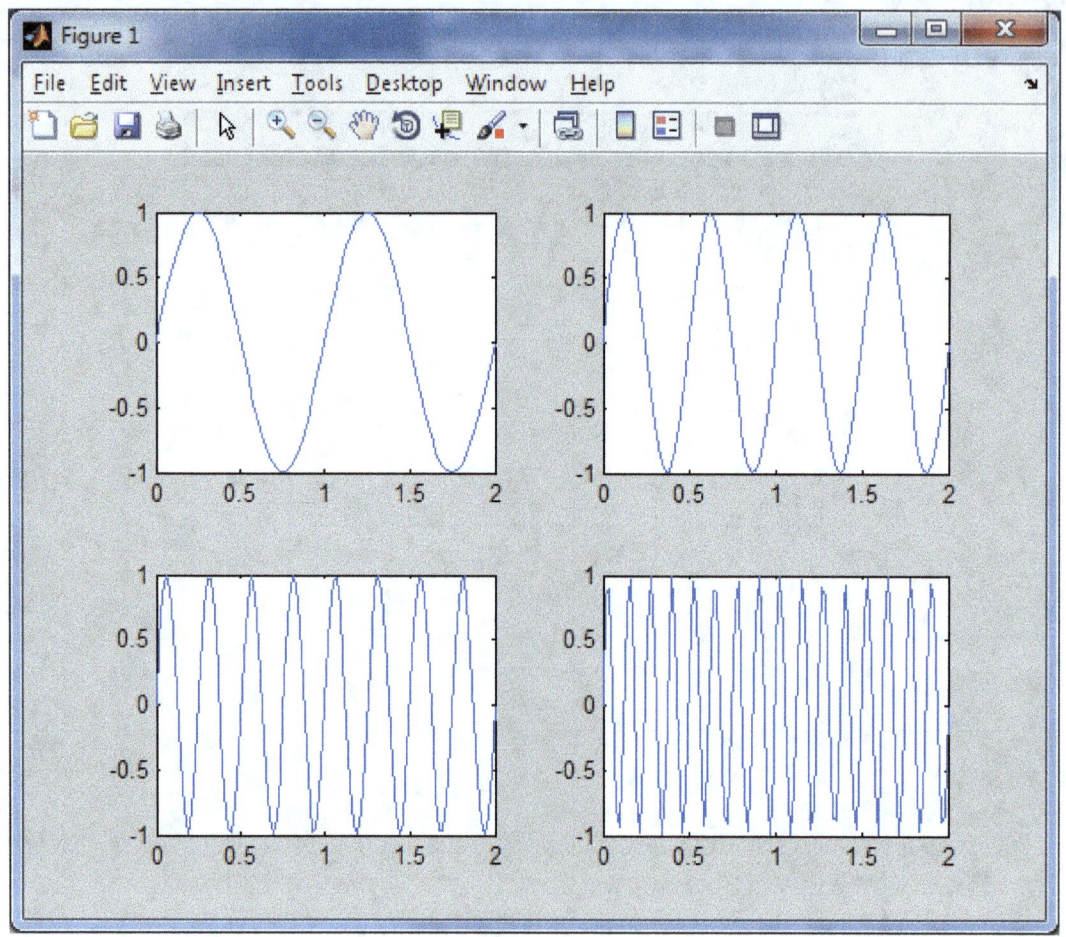

Figure-4.20

The commands xlabel, ylabel, title and axis used for PLOT and STEM commands can be used separately for each subgraph, and they are written after the PLOT and STEM commands which are written after SUBPLOT command.

Example-4.11:

```
close all;
t = linspace(0,2,100);
f=1;
y1 = sin(2*pi*f*t);
subplot(2,2,1);
plot(t,y1);
xlabel('f=1');
ylabel('y_1');
title('y_1');

f=2;
y2 = sin(2*pi*f*t);
subplot(2,2,2);
plot(t,y2);
xlabel('f=2');
ylabel('y_2');
title('y_2');

f=4;
y3 = sin(2*pi*f*t);
subplot(2,2,3);
plot(t,y3);
xlabel('f=4');
ylabel('y_3');
title('y_3');

subplot(2,2,4);
f=8;
y4 = sin(2*pi*f*t);
plot(t,y4);
xlabel('f=8');
ylabel('y_4');
title('y_4');
```

Figure-4.21

When the program in Figure-4.21 is run, we get the graph in Figure-4.22.

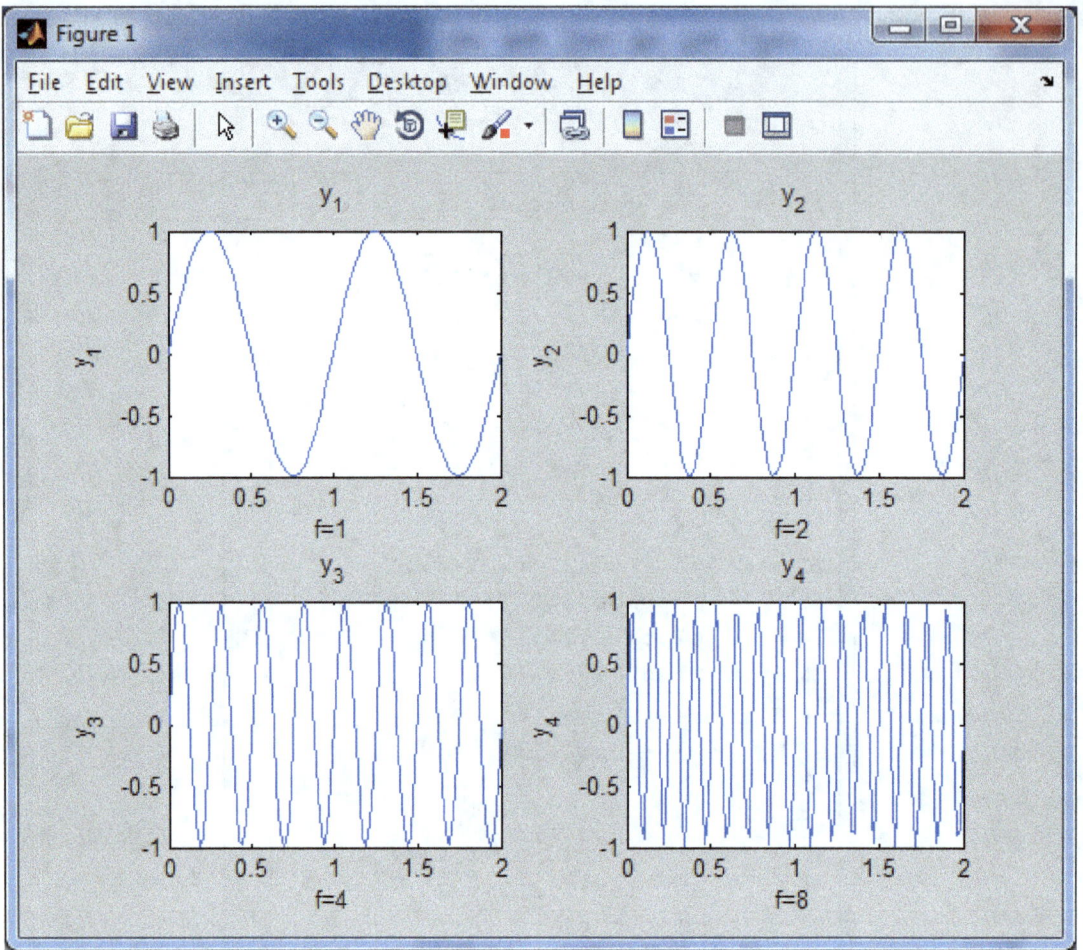

Figure-4.22

4.3 FIGURE Command

The FIGURE command is used to open a new figure window or to make one of the open windows the current window. It is used as

$$\texttt{figure} \text{ or } \texttt{figure(n)}$$

The FIGURE(n) command is used to make the figure with figure number n the current figure and new graphic is drawn on the current figure.

Example-4.12: The use of figure command is illustrated in the MATLAB program in Figure-4.23.

```
1    close all;
2
3    x1 = [1 3 5 7];
4    y1 = [2 4 6 5];
5    plot (x1, y1);    % the graph is drawn on figure-1
6
7    figure; % a new figure is opened with number 2
8    x2 = [1 3 5 7];
9    y2 = [3 5 8 2];
10   plot (x2, y2) ;
11
12   figure; % a new figure is opened with number 3
13   x3 = [1 3 5 7];
14   y3 = [1 6 2 4];
15   plot (x3,y3);
16
17   figure (1); % the next graph is drawn on figure-1
18   hold on;
19   x4 = [1 3 5 7];
20   y4 = [4 7 1 6] ;
21   plot (x4,y4,'r');
22
23   figure(3); % figure-3 is the current figure
24   hold on;
25   plot(x4, y4, 'g'); % graph is drawn on figure-3
```

Figure-4.23

Bibliography

1) https://www.mathworks.com/help/MATLAB/

2) B. R. Hunt, G. J. Stuck et all, A Guide to MATLAB: For Beginners and Experienced Users, Cambridge University Press; ISBN-10 : 0521615658

www.ingramcontent.com/pod-product-compliance
Lightning Source LLC
Chambersburg PA
CBHW062117220526
45471CB00010B/3762